Voices 6.º ano
Língua Estrangeira Moderna - Inglês

Vera Lúcia Rauta

Bacharel em Ciências Econômicas pela Universidade Federal do Paraná.

Pós-Graduada em Pedagogia Escolar e em Ensino de Línguas Estrangeiras Modernas.

Certificado internacional em Língua Inglesa pela Universidade de Cambridge (Inglaterra) e em Língua Francesa pela Universidade de Nancy (França).

Tradutora de livros na área médica.

Coautora de livros didáticos para o Ensino Fundamental e Educação de Jovens e Adultos.

Professora de Língua Inglesa e Francesa das redes pública e particular de ensino do estado do Paraná.

1ª Edição
Curitiba, 2012

BASE EDITORIAL

Dados para Catalogação
Bibliotecária responsável: Izabel Cristina de Souza
CRB-9/633 – Curitiba, PR.

R249v
Rauta, Vera Lúcia
  Voices : 6º ano : manual do professor / Vera Lúcia Rauta. – Curitiba : Base Editorial, 2012.
  208p. : il. col. ; 28 cm. - (Língua estrangeira moderna : inglês ; v. 1)

  ISBN : 978-85-7905-927-8 (professor)
  ISBN : 978-85-7905-926-1 (aluno)
  Inclui bibliografia

  1. Língua inglesa (Ensino fundamental) - Estudo e ensino.
  I. Título. II. Série.

CDD 21. ed.
372.6521
428.24

Voices – 6º ano
Copyright – Vera Lúcia Rauta
2012

Conselho editorial
Mauricio Carvalho
Oralda A. de Souza
Renato Guimarães
Dimitri Vasic

Gerência editorial
Eloiza Jaguelte Silva

Editora
Grenilza Maria Lis Zabot

Editora assistente
Lúcia Chueire Lopes

Coordenação de produção editorial
Marline Meurer Paitra

Assistência de produção
José Cabral Lima Jr.
Rafael Ricardo Silva

Iconografia
Osmarina F. Tosta
Ana Cláudia Dias

Revisão
Caibar Pereira Magalhães Junior
Juliana Bassichetti Martins

Revisão de Língua Inglesa
Nicholas Paul Farmer

Leitura comparativa
Lincoln Cardoso da Silva

Licenciamento de texto
Valquiria Salviato Guariente
Liana Bisolo Warmling

Projeto gráfico e diagramação
Labores Graphici

Ilustrações
Carlos Cesar Salvadori
Ricardo Luiz Enz

Capa
Labores Graphici – Carlos Cesar Salvadori
Fotos (da esquerda para a direita): © .shock/Fotolia.com; © Monkey Business/Fotolia.com; © Monkey Business/Fotolia.com; © Monkey Business/Fotolia.com; © Scott Griessel/Fotolia.com; © PicturenetCorp/Fotolia.com; © Anatoliy Samara/Fotolia.com; © Jacek Chabraszewski/Fotolia.com; © Yuri Arcurs/Fotolia.com; Golden Pixels LLC/Shutterstock.

CTP, Impressão e Acabamento IBEP Gráfica
41968

Base Editorial Ltda.
Rua Antônio Martin de Araújo, 343 • Jardim Botânico • CEP 80210-050
Tel.: (41) 3264-4114 • Fax: (41) 3264-8471 • Curitiba • Paraná
Site: www.baseeditora.com.br • *E-mail*: baseeditora@baseeditora.com.br

Apresentação

Querido aluno:

Inglês. A língua do mundo. A língua global. A língua internacional.

Quantas vezes você tem ouvido ou lido essa expressão ultimamente?

O inglês tornou-se uma necessidade básica na sua vida e na vida de todos os que habitam o planeta Terra. E você sabe por quê?

Quando você está viajando e não consegue encontrar o seu hotel, quando é abordado por alguém no estrangeiro, ou por um estrangeiro no Brasil, que pede sua ajuda, verá que o inglês é a língua comum entre os turistas do mundo todo. Você precisará dele para receber os turistas que virão ao Brasil para a Copa do Mundo de 2014 e para as Olimpíadas de 2016.

Se você estuda, precisará do inglês para o vestibular, para uma pós-graduação, para um MBA, mestrado ou doutorado.

Se você observar os jornais, poderá verificar quantos anúncios de empregos incluem em suas exigências que os profissionais dominem pelo menos um idioma. E que idioma é esse? O inglês.

O inglês é o meio de comunicação internacional entre países que trocam informações e fecham negócios.

O inglês também nos insere em novas culturas e tradições.

O conhecimento global é produzido em inglês: filmes, inovações tecnológicas, arte, artigos científicos.

O inglês é o idioma da internet que nos possibilita encontrar informações e entrar em contato com pessoas que possivelmente nunca conheceríamos.

Além disso, o inglês permeia boa parte da sua vida cotidiana: nas músicas que você ouve, nos filmes que vê em inglês com legendas em português, nos jogos eletrônicos e da internet, nas redes sociais de que você faz parte.

Aprender o inglês é tudo isso e muito mais.

Por isso, convidamos você para aprender o inglês e abrir um leque de opções infinitas em sua vida. Esta coleção lhe dará a voz necessária para que você se torne um cidadão do mundo globalizado. Mundo esse em que as pessoas trocam experiências, vivem uma realidade mais moderna, mais igualitária e solidária.

Bom trabalho!

A autora.

Contents

Unit	Grammar	Vocabulary	Function
1 Around the world Page 6	Present: to be What's your name? My name's... I'm... Where are you from? I'm from... Question words: what, where	Greetings Introductions Countries Nationalities	Greeting people Introducing yourself Asking someone's name Asking someone where he's/she's from
2 In the classroom Page 16	Present: to be What's this? This is my/your... What's your favorite subject? It is.../ It's... Imperative (affirmative and negative forms) Preposition of time: on	Classroom objects School subjects Days of the week	Talking about classroom objects Talking about possessions Describing a class schedule Talking about favorite subjects Practicing the language used in the classroom

Review Unit 1 (U1 + U2) Page 26

Unit	Grammar	Vocabulary	Function
3 At school Page 28	Present: to be Where is...? It's... How do you spell...? Question word: how	Cardinal numbers from 1 to 30 Rooms at school The alphabet	Asking about rooms at school and answering Spelling names and surnames
4 My family Page 38	Present: to be Affirmative and Interrogative forms Who's this/that? Who are these/those? Question word: who, how many	Family members Professions	Identifying members of the family Introducing and asking about the family Talking and describing other people Confirming identities Answering about professions

Review Unit 2 (U3 + U4) Page 48

Unit	Grammar	Vocabulary	Function
5 Let's eat — Page 50	Present: to be Negative form Present: to like Affirmative form Singular/plural forms Question word: how much (price)	Food and drink Meals Food at home/at school Prices Money Cardinal numbers from 40 to 100	Identifying and talking about food Talking about favorite food at school/at home Asking about prices and answering Talking about money
6 How is the weather? — Page 60	Present: to be Which is...? Present: to like I like... Possessive adjectives Question words: which	Personal objects Clothes/Colors Weather Months Ordinal numbers from 1 to 30	Talking about personal objects Identifying different clothes Describing colors and clothes Talking about the weather and months of the year Talking about clothes for each type of weather
Review Unit 3 (U5 + U6) — Page 72			
7 Around town — Page 74	Present: there to be There is.../There are... Interrogative, Affirmative and Negative forms Prepositions of place: in, on	Places in town Parts of the house Furniture Time	Locating places and buildings in town Identifying parts of the house Talking about rooms and furniture Asking and telling the time
8 Talents — Page 86	Can (ability) Interrogative, Affirmative and Negative forms	Sports Musical instruments Languages Action verbs Pets	Identifying talents and abilities Talking about abilities Expressing preferences about pets

Review Unit 4 (U7 + U8) — Page 96

Workbook – Pages 98-121
Projects – Pages 124-127
Glossary – Pages 130-135
Reading is Fun – Pages 138-142

How do you say... in English? Pages 122-123
Grammar Points – Pages 128-129
Listening scripts – Pages 136-137
References – Pages 143-144

This icon indicates related digital content.

UNIT 1

AROUND THE WORLD

- Present (to be) – Greetings and Introductions

WARM-UP: Why is it important to attend a school?
Discuss it with your classmates and your teacher.

Read

SCHOOLS AROUND THE WORLD

1. Let's take a look at these pictures. What can you see?

a) Students at school in London, England. 2008.

b) Students at school in Cairo, Egypt. 2009.

2. Where are these schools? Use the subtitles below the pictures to help you.

_____

3. Now look at the pictures again. What differences and similarities can you see?

_____

SCHOOLS IN BRAZIL

1. Now let's look at some schools in Brazil. Are our schools similar or different? Do they have anything in common?

   a) Escola indígena da Aldeia Guarani Tenonde Porã. Parelheiros, São Paulo (SP). 2010.

   b) Escola na Comunidade Bacucuara. Rio Aracá (AM). 2008.

2. These schools are in Brazil. Where are they? Use the subtitles below the pictures to help you.

Exchanging ideas

- The pictures on pages 6 and 7 show schools in different countries and in Brazil. Compare the pictures. How are the schools different? What about your school?
- Which school do you prefer? Why?
- In your opinion, what makes a good school?
- What difference does going to school make?

Don't miss!

<www.epals.com>. *Site* que promove a comunicação entre professores e alunos no mundo inteiro. Acesso em: 27 jun. 2011.

WENDEL, Fernanda. **Estudar**: qual o segredo? Como ir bem na escola aprendendo de verdade. Editora Ática, 2011. Um livro que descreve atitudes que podem ajudá-lo a melhorar seu rendimento escolar.

DUNNE, Brendan; NEWTON, Robin. **Teamwork**. Richmond Publishing, 2011. História de duas meninas que são esquecidas dentro de um museu e notam que há bandidos no local tentanto roubar o maior diamante do mundo.

Listen

1. Look at the world map and the people on it. Listen and try to point to them.

> Hi, I'm David.
>
> Hello! My name's Kazuki. What's your name?
>
> Hi, I'm Silvia.
>
> Hello, everybody. My name's Gabriela.

TRACK 2

Remember that:

I am = I'm
My name is = My name's
What is = What's

2. There are more students at this school. Listen and repeat.

TRACK 3

This is Ricardo.   This is Sarah.   This is Lyndon.   This is Laura.   This is Cate.

Speak

1. Listen and read. TRACK 4

- I'm from Brazil. Where are you from?
- I'm from Brazil, too.
- I'm from the United States of America. I'm from the USA. (Also referred to as **the United States, the U.S., the USA or America**)
- I'm from Japan.

Pronunciation

I'**m** **f**rom: Close your mouth when you pronounce m.
Unite**d**: There's no vowel after d.
States: Sound s.

2. Listen and repeat. TRACK 5

Hi! I'm Ricardo and I'm from Brazil.

Sarah is from England.   Lyndon is from South Africa.   Laura is from Argentina.   Cate is from Australia.

3. Now it's your turn. Read, listen and speak.

- Hi! My name's Gabriela and I'm from Brazil. Where are you from?
- Hello, Gabriela. I'm Kazuki and I'm from Japan.

9

Grammar points

1. Look at the students. They're speaking English. What are they talking about? Read the dialogues.

- Where are you from, Sarah?
- I'm from London. I'm English.

- Hi, Laura. Are you from Buenos Aires?
- Yes, I am. I'm Argentinean.

- I'm from São Paulo. I'm Brazilian. Where are you from?
- I'm from Tokyo. I'm Japanese.

- I'm not from England. I'm from Washington, D.C.. I'm American.
- I'm not American. I'm Australian. I'm from Sydney.

2. Look closely. Read the dialogues above again. Then complete the table below.

Full Forms	Short Forms
What is your name?	What's your name?
My name is Kazuki.	My name's Kazuki.
I am Silvia.	
	I'm from Japan.
I am American.	
I am not English.	

Vocabulary

1. Look at these flags. What are their corresponding countries? Match.

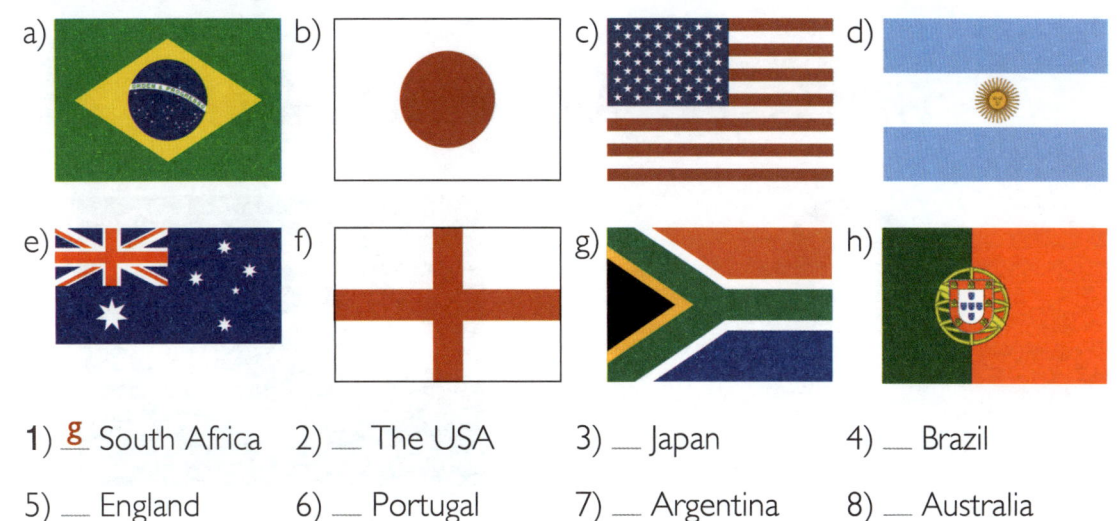

a) b) c) d)

e) f) g) h)

1) _g_ South Africa   2) ___ The USA   3) ___ Japan   4) ___ Brazil

5) ___ England   6) ___ Portugal   7) ___ Argentina   8) ___ Australia

2. Go back to page 9. Check where the students are from. Look at the nationalities below. Complete the sentences.

> Brazilian – Japanese – South African – Australian
> English – Portuguese – American – Argentinean

a) Ricardo is **Brazilian**.   b) Sarah is _____.

c) Lyndon is _____.   d) David is _____.

e) Laura is _____.   f) Cate is _____.

g) Kazuki is _____.

3. Tell a classmate your name, the country you're from and your nationality. Then write the sentences here.

_____

_____

Remember that:

Countries and nationalities are written with capital letters.
Japan = Japanese   Brazil = Brazilian
Capital letter = upper case = A   lower case = a

11

Write

Read

1.

THAT'S ME AND MY SCHOOL

I'm Ricardo.

I'm from Brazil.
I'm Brazilian.

This is my school in Brazil.

These are my friends.

This is my teacher.

This is my classroom.

2. In the poster, Ricardo wrote these words:

<u>This</u> is my school in Brazil.

<u>These</u> are my friends.

<u>That's</u> me and my school.

Remember that:

The underlined words are demonstrative pronouns.

3. What do you need to make a poster?

a) Provide a picture of your school. What's your school called?
_____

b) Provide a picture of your friends and you. What are their names?
_____

c) Provide a picture of your teacher. What is your English teacher's name?
_____

d) Provide a picture of your classroom. Is it a small or big classroom?
_____

e) Provide other pictures like: rooms in your school and people who work there or even a quotation about schools. Here is one of them. Read it now.

> The difference between school and life? In school, you're taught a lesson and then given a test. In life you're given a test that teaches you a lesson.
>
> (Tom Bodett)

Exchanging ideas

- Talk about the quotation with your friends.
- Do you agree with this quotation?

4. Now you can make your poster. Use the hints on page 12 to help you.

Click

<http://cyberschoolbus.un.org/>. Acesso em: 19 jun. 2011. *Website* da Organização das Nações Unidas sobre assuntos globais para alunos de 5 a 18 anos e professores.

<www.studentsoftheworld.info/menu_pres.html>. Acesso em: 19 jun. 2011. *Site* de uma associação francesa sem fins lucrativos cujo objetivo é abrir as portas da cultura humana para pessoas jovens.

Let's have fun!

famous people

1. Look at the secret code. Change numbers into letters. Then read the sentences.

1 A	2 B	3 C	4 D	5 E	6 F	7 G
8 H	9 I	10 J	11 K	12 L	13 M	14 N
15 O	16 P	17 Q	18 R	19 S	20 T	21 U
22 V	23 W	24 X	25 Y	26 Z		

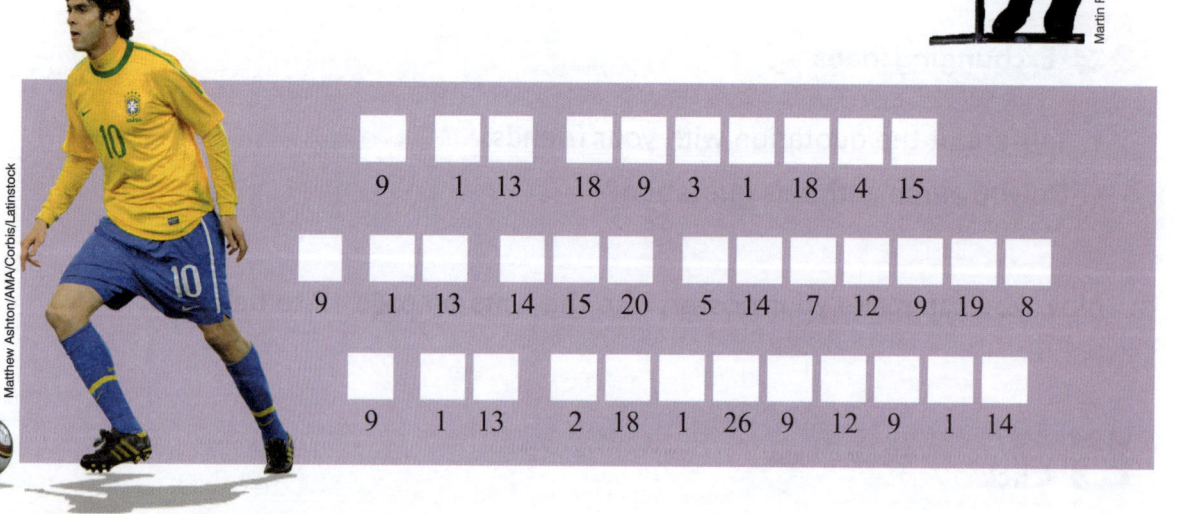

M Y **N A M E** **I S** **M A D O N N A**
13 25 14 1 13 5   9 19   13 1 4 15 14 14 1

I A M **F R O M** **T H E** **U S A**
9 1 13   6 18 15 13   20 8 5   21 19 1

I A M **A M E R I C A N**
9 1 13   1 13 5 18 9 3 1 14

I A M **R I C A R D O**
9 1 13   18 9 3 1 18 4 15

I A M **N O T** **E N G L I S H**
9 1 13   14 15 20   5 14 7 12 9 19 8

I A M **B R A Z I L I A N**
9 1 13   2 18 1 26 9 12 9 1 14

Remember that:

I am – Affirmative full form

I am not – Negative full form

Exercise the mind

1. Look how we say "Where are you from?" in other languages.

   a) Where are you from?

   b) Doko kara desu ka?

   c) De onde você é?

   d) ¿De dónde es usted?

   e) Woher kommst Du?

   f) Di dove sei?

Click

Se você quiser verificar a pergunta *Where are you from?* em outras línguas, acesse: <www.ominiglot.com/language/phrases/wherefrom.htm>.
Acesso em: 19 jun. 2001.

2. Do you know the languages in exercise 1?

   What languages are they?

   a) **English**
   b) _____
   c) _____
   d) _____
   e) _____
   f) _____

Exchanging ideas

- And you? Where are you from in Brazil?
- Are Brazilians similar? Talk about it.
- Are Brazilians different? Talk about it.
- Do Brazilians have something in common?

UNIT 2

IN THE CLASSROOM

• Present (to be) – School subjects – Language used in the classroom

WARM-UP: What is an international school?
Would you like to study in an international school?

Read

1. Read the school subjects. What words can you understand?

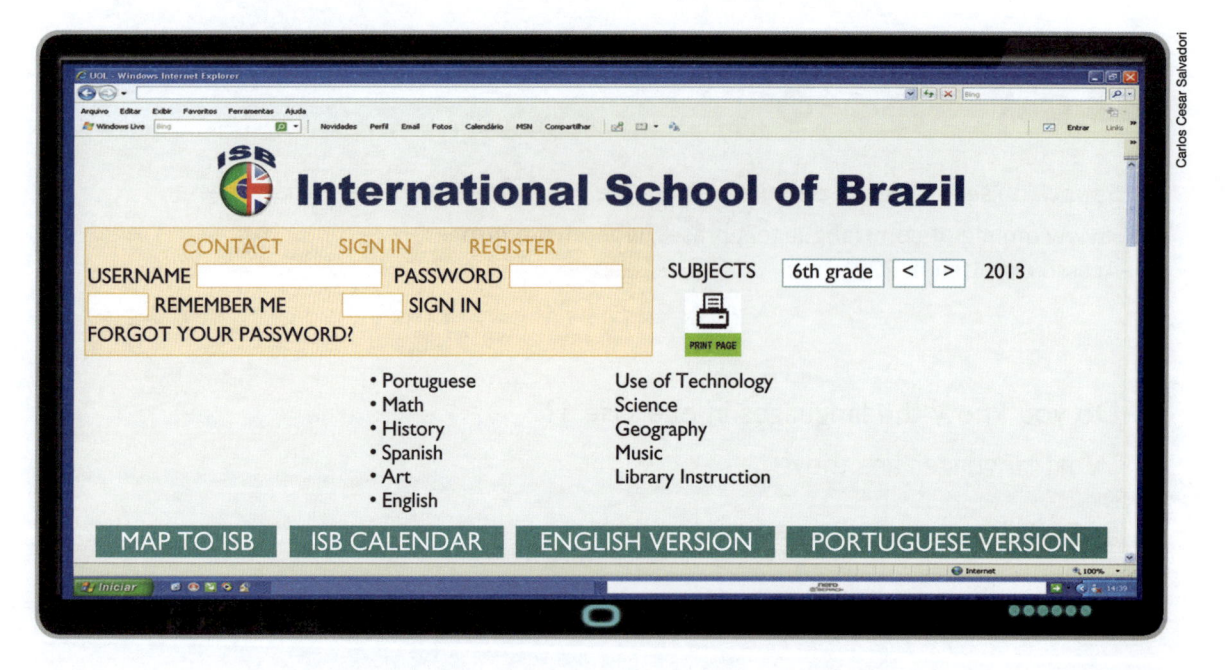

International School of Brazil

CONTACT SIGN IN REGISTER
USERNAME PASSWORD
REMEMBER ME SIGN IN
FORGOT YOUR PASSWORD?

SUBJECTS 6th grade < > 2013

PRINT PAGE

- Portuguese
- Math
- History
- Spanish
- Art
- English

Use of Technology
Science
Geography
Music
Library Instruction

MAP TO ISB | ISB CALENDAR | ENGLISH VERSION | PORTUGUESE VERSION

2. Do you have similar subjects in your school? What subjects do you have at school?

Click

Há algumas escolas internacionais no Brasil. Você conhece alguma delas? Se não conhece, entre nestes dois *sites* e observe como elas funcionam.

<www.iscbrazil.com/>. Acesso em: 6 jun. 2011. *Website* da International School of Curitiba / Escola Internacional de Curitiba, no Paraná.

<www.bischool.com.br/index.php>. Acesso em: 6 jun. 2011. *Website* da Brasília International School / Escola Internacional de Brasília, no Distrito Federal.

3. Look at the students' schedule in the International School of Brazil.

6th Grade Schedule							
	Sunday	Monday	Tuesday	Wednesday	Thursday	Friday	Saturday
1	No class	Math	Use of Technology	Portuguese	English	History	No class
2	\	Portuguese	History	Music	Math	Spanish	\
3	/	Geography	Art	English	Science	Music	/
	\	Break	Break	Break	Break	Break	\
4	/	Science	English	Physical Education	Math	Use of Technology	/
5	\	English	Math	Use of Technology	Portuguese	Portuguese	\
6	/	Library Instruction	Science	Library Instruction	Art	Geography	/

4. Now write the schedule you have at your school.

Sunday	Monday	Tuesday	Wednesday	Thursday	Friday	Saturday

Exchanging ideas

- Check the schedules in exercise 3 and 4. Do you have a similar or a different schedule at your school?

Click

<www.manythings.org/hmf/hm-subjects.html>. Acesso em: 12 jul. 2011. (Você pode jogar forca (*hangman*) neste *site*. O jogo é sobre as disciplinas escolares).

Don't miss!

ZIRALDO. **Uma professora muito maluquinha**. São Paulo: Melhoramentos, 2008. (História de uma professora que se torna fundamental na vida de seus alunos).

Listen

1. Listen and repeat.

a) **WHEN YOU NEED HELP** — TRACK 6

Excuse me, how do you say "caneta" in English?

book/substantivo, livro; verbo, reservar.

What does "book" mean?

Sorry. Can you repeat that, please?

b) **LANGUAGE USED IN THE CLASSROOM** — TRACK 7

Open your books.

Close your books.

Listen to the CD.

Let's check the activity.

2. Now look at the students in the classroom.

a) TRACK 8

Are you ready?

No. Just a minute, please.

b) TRACK 9

You go first.

Ok, I'll go first.

Why learn?

Excuse me, **sorry** and **please** are polite words. These words show respect and consideration for the people around us.

Speak

1. Look at the scene. What are David and Ricardo doing?

2. Now listen to the conversation.

David: It's Tuesday today.
Ricardo: Yes. History class now. My favorite subject is history. What about you?
David: Use of Technology. I like computers, cell phones, tablets…
Ricardo: Tab… can you repeat, please?
David: Tablet.
Ricardo: Tablet. What does "tablet" mean?
David: It's a small portable computer with a touchscreen.
Ricardo: Oh, I see. Thanks for your help.
David: You're welcome.
Silvia: Ok, students! Open your books to page 10, exercise 2. Are you ready? Listen to the CD, please…

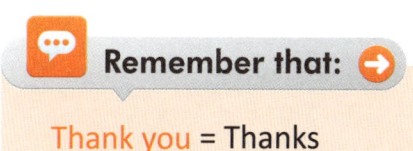

Pronunciation

- Th

Practice: *Th*anks. / *Th*ank you.

Remember that:

Thank you = Thanks

3. Listen and repeat. Then practice the dialogue.

Gabriela: What's your favorite subject, Kazuki?
Kazuki: My favorite subject is science. What about you?
Gabriela: My favorite subject is Portuguese.

Grammar points

1. Here is the students' schedule for Monday. Read the dialogue.

Cate: What's the day today, Lyndon?

Lyndon: Today is Monday. It is Monday.

Cate: Math is on Monday.

Lyndon: Yes, it is.

Cate: What about music?

Lyndon: It is not on Monday. It's on Wednesday and Friday. Is music your favorite subject?

Cate: Yes, it is. I like it a lot.

	Monday
1	Math
2	Portuguese
3	Geography
	Break
4	Science
5	English
6	Library Instruction

2. Look closely at the dialogue again. What is the relation between <u>today</u> and <u>it</u>?

_____

3. Look for other examples using "it". Write them.

_____

4. Now complete the table below with the verb **to be** in the full and in the short forms.

Full Form	Short Form
I am Laura.	I'm Laura.
I am not American.	
It is on Monday.	
	It isn't on Monday.

Remember that:

- We use the preposition **ON** before the days of the week: Geography is **on** Monday and **on** Friday.
- We use capital letters with the days of the week: The music concert is on <u>S</u>unday.

Vocabulary

1. Look at Laura and Kazuki. Look at the backpacks. Label the things with the words from the boxes.

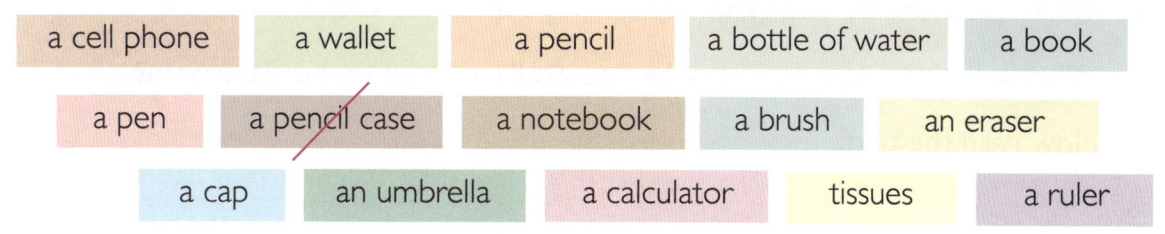

   a cell phone | a wallet | a pencil | a bottle of water | a book

   a pen | a pencil case | a notebook | a brush | an eraser

   a cap | an umbrella | a calculator | tissues | a ruler

2. Listen and check. TRACK 12

   1. a pencil case
   2.
   3.
   4.
   5.
   6.
   7.
   8.
   9.
   10.
   11.
   12.
   13.
   14.
   15.

3. And you? What's in your backpack?
   Write the objects here.

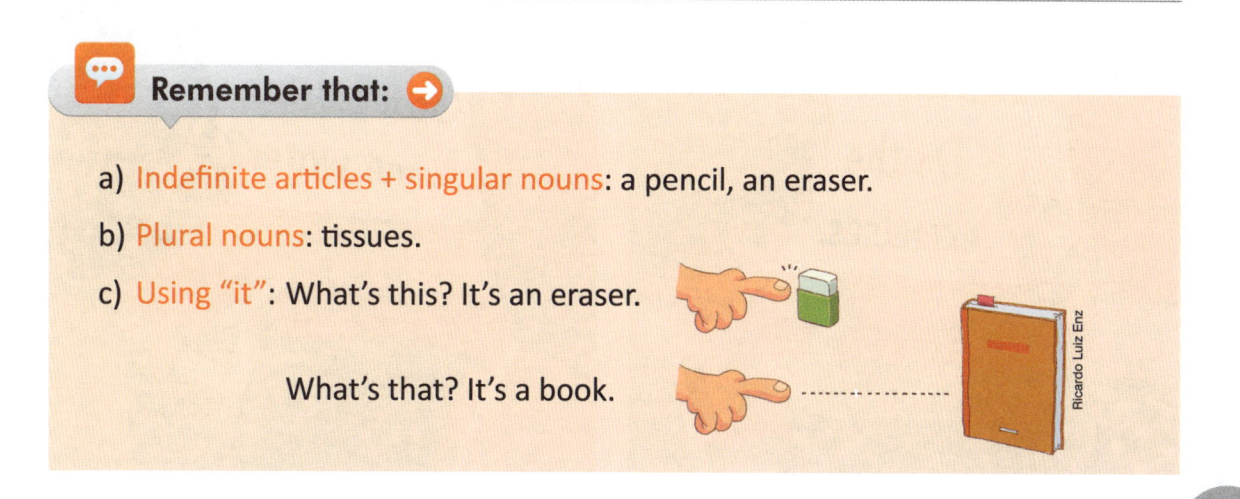

   _____

Remember that:

a) **Indefinite articles + singular nouns**: a pencil, an eraser.

b) **Plural nouns**: tissues.

c) **Using "it"**: What's this? It's an eraser.

   What's that? It's a book.

Write

1. Look at the pictures below. What are the students doing?
2. What questions do you generally ask in your English class?
3. What questions does your teacher generally ask you in the classroom?
4. Now read the text.

IN THE CLASSROOM

The students are in the classroom now. Mrs. Costa is there too. It's English class. The students are writing important sentences and questions they can use in the classroom to communicate.

May I go to the toilet?

Look at me, please!

Do the exercises.

Can I drink some water?

Ricardo Luiz Enz

5. Now look at the students' classroom. What are they saying? Can you guess the meaning of them?

- Pay attention, please!
- May I open the window, please?
- May I clean the board?
- Can you step aside, please?
- May I use the computer?

6. Look at these sentences. They are in the imperative form.

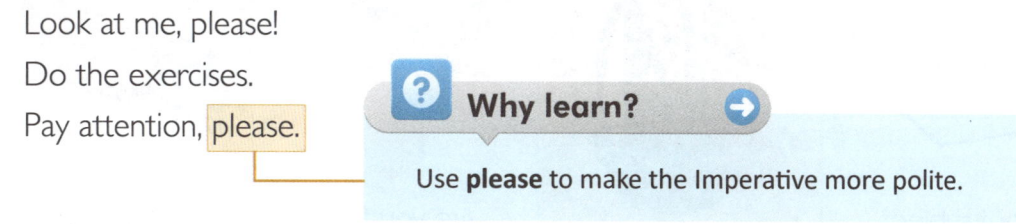

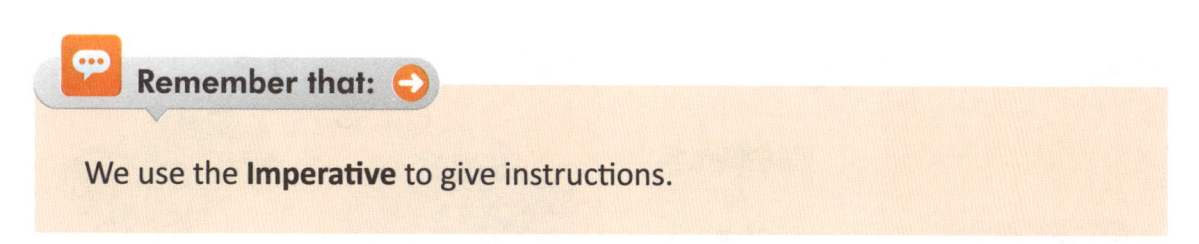

Look at me, please!
Do the exercises.
Pay attention, please.

Why learn?

Use **please** to make the Imperative more polite.

Remember that:

We use the **Imperative** to give instructions.

7. Now it's your turn. Write your questions and sentences. Put them on the wall. Use them in your English class.

23

Let's have fun!

let's play this game!

1 START

2 What's this?

3 What's your name?

4 What's this?

5 Are you from Japan?

6 Are you from Brazil?

7 TUESDAY / Science / Music / Geography / Math / Use of Technology
Is music on Tuesday?

8 Where are you from?

9 What subject is it?

10 Is this a cap?

11 Are you from São Paulo?

12 Is this an eraser?

13 Are you Brazilian?

14 Are you Australian?

15 FRIDAY / Art / Music / English / Math
Is history on Friday?

16 FINISH

24

Exercise the mind →

What is peace? Do you have peace? What about peace in the classroom?

PEACE BEGINS IN THE CLASSROOM

Sometimes conflict is inevitable.

When you are in the classroom and there's conflict involving you and another student do you try to:

CONTROL YOUR EMOTION AND WALK AWAY?

SHARE SCHOOL OBJECTS WHENEVER IT IS POSSIBLE?

LEARN TO APOLOGIZE?

GET HELP FROM YOUR FRIENDS AND YOUR TEACHER?

Exchanging ideas →

- What about you?
- What do you do to promote peace in the classroom?
- Read Gandhi's quotation. Do you agree with him?

"The weak never forgive. Forgiveness is the attribute of the strong." (Mahatma Gandhi, 1869-1948)

Click →

<http://letras.terra.com.br/john-lennon/90/traducao.html>. Acesso em: 8 jun. 2011.

"Imagine" – Letra de John Lennon. Você pode ouvir a música, ver a tradução e ainda assistir ao vídeo com John Lennon.

Review 1: UNIT 1/2

1. Look at the pictures. Write **this**, **that**, **these** or **those**.

a) Look at **those** English books.

b) _____ is my teacher.

c) Is _____ my umbrella?

d) _____ are my tissues.

2. Write the indefinite articles, **a** or **an**.

a) **an** umbrella   b) _____ pencil case

c) _____ brush   d) _____ wallet

e) _____ eraser   f) _____ American

g) _____ book   h) _____ ruler

i) _____ art book   j) _____ minute

k) _____ English class   l) _____ country

3. Unscramble the letters to form the days of the week.

   a) **Wednesday**
      d s w a y e n e d

   b) __ __ __ __ __ __ __ __
      h s d t u r a y

   c) __ __ __ __ __ __
      y u d s n a

   d) __ __ __ __ __ __
      a e t d y u s

   e) __ __ __ __ __ __
      d m o y a n

   f) __ __ __ __ __ __
      y i r a d f

   g) __ __ __ __ __ __ __ __
      a a y u d r t s

4. Unscramble the words to make sentences or questions.

   a) **How do you say "computador" in English (?)**
      / ? / say / How / English / do / in / you / "computador"

   b) _____
      /. / your / please / books / Close / , /

   c) _____
      / ? / you /Can /, / please / repeat / that

   d) _____
      / ? / does / mean / What / "tablet"

5. Write the sentences and questions in the contracted form.

   a) What is the day today?
      What's the day today?

   b) It is not on Wednesday.

   _____

   c) It is math.

   _____

   d) What is your favorite school subject?

   _____

   e) That is a wallet.

   _____

UNIT 3

AT SCHOOL

- Present (to be) – Rooms at school – Prepositions of place

WARM-UP: Do you have a student card?
What do you do with a student card?

Read

1. Look at the students' cards below.

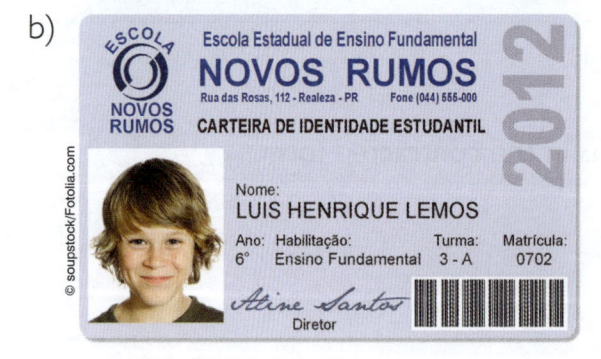

   a)

   b)

2. Now answer the questions about the students' cards.

   a) What can you see on the student's cards?

   _____

   b) What kind of information can you see on the students' cards?

   _____

3. Look at the picture on page 29. What's going on?

4. Now read the dialogue.

At the secretary's office

Miss Santos: Hi! May I help you?
Sarah: Yes, please. I need my student card.
Miss Santos: Ok. What's your full name?
Sarah: Sarah Gibbs.
Miss Santos: Let's check. How do you spell your last name?
Sarah: It's G-I-B-B-S.
Miss Santos: Ok, thank you. Where are you from, Sarah?
Sarah: I'm from London, England.
Miss Santos: OK, Sarah. Here's your student card. Keep it safe, right?
Sarah: Ok. Thank you.
Miss Santos: You're welcome.

Remember that:

Mr. = Men
Miss = Single women
Mrs. = Married women
Ms. = Single or married women

5. Now look at Sarah's student card.

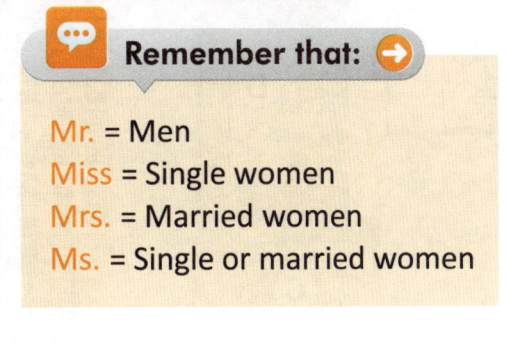

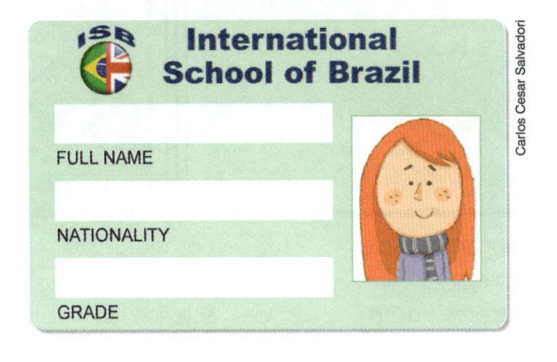

Exchanging ideas

- What kind of information does the student's card contain?
- Do you have a similar card at your school?
- What can you do if you have a student card?

Listen

Rooms at school

1. Look at the students' school below. 🎵 TRACK 13

A – principal's office	E – computer lab	H – classroom	K – gym
B – secretary's office	F – music room	I – boys' room	L – art room
C – teachers' room	G – science lab	J – girls' room	M – cafeteria
D – library			

Exchanging ideas

- Do you ever talk to the principal of your school?
- Is there a place for you to eat at your school?
- Does your school look the same or different from the one in the picture?

Speak

1. Listen to the dialogue. What's Laura's problem?

Laura is at school, but she's lost. She meets Miss Santos and asks for help.

Miss Santos: Hi, Laura. Are you ok?

Laura: No, I'm not. I'm lost. Where's the library?

Miss Santos: It's between the teachers' room and the computer lab.

Laura: Ok, thank you. And where's the science lab?

Miss Santos: It's next to your classroom. And the library is across from your classroom.

BETWEEN   NEXT TO   ACROSS FROM

2. Now practice the dialogue with your friends.

3. Change roles. Use other rooms from the school floor plan on page 30 to practice the dialogue.

Grammar points

1. Listen and repeat the alphabet. **TRACK 14**

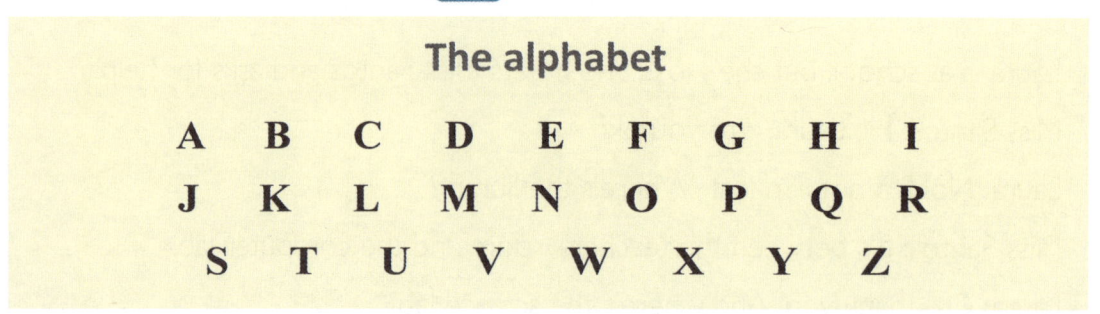

   The alphabet

   A B C D E F G H I
   J K L M N O P Q R
   S T U V W X Y Z

2. Spell your full name.

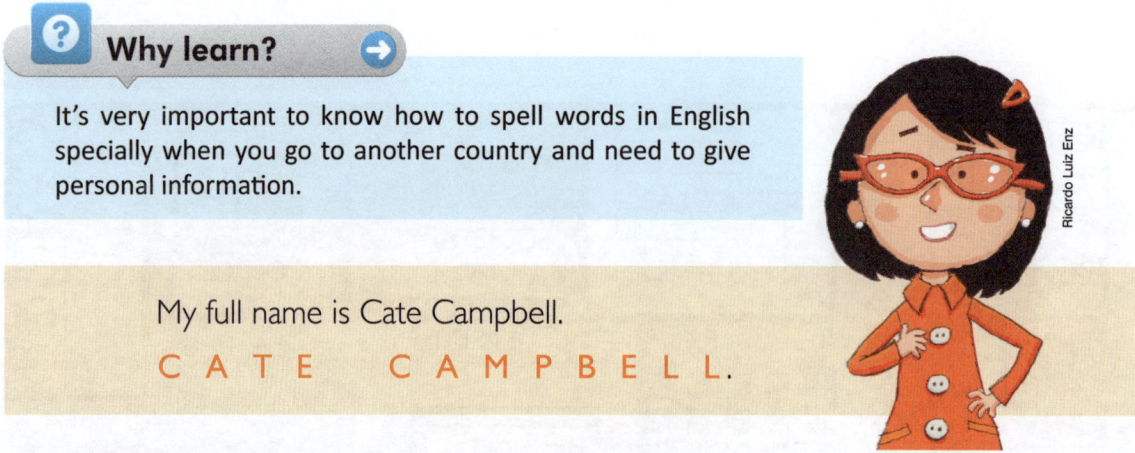

   Why learn?

   It's very important to know how to spell words in English specially when you go to another country and need to give personal information.

   My full name is Cate Campbell.
   C A T E   C A M P B E L L.

3. Tell your full name to a friend.

4. Read the dialogue below.

   How do you spell your full name?

   L-Y-N-D-O-N B-E-N-T.

5. Now practice the dialogue with a friend.

6. Change roles. Now listen and write four school rooms. **TRACK 15**

   a) ___ ___ ___ ___ ___ ___ ___ ___ ___
   b) ___ ___ ___ ___ ___ ___ ___ ___
   c) ___ ___ ___ ___ ___ ___ ___
   d) ___ ___ ___

32

Vocabulary

1. Listen and repeat the numbers from 0 to 30. (TRACK 16)

Numbers from 1 to 30

0 – oh / zero	10 – ten	20 – twenty
1 – one	11 – eleven	21 – twenty-one
2 – two	12 – twelve	22 – twenty-two
3 – three	13 – thirteen	23 – twenty-three
4 – four	14 – fourteen	24 – twenty-four
5 – five	15 – fifteen	25 – twenty-five
6 – six	16 – sixteen	26 – twenty-six
7 – seven	17 – seventeen	27 – twenty-seven
8 – eight	18 – eighteen	28 – twenty-eight
9 – nine	19 – nineteen	29 – twenty-nine
		30 – thirty

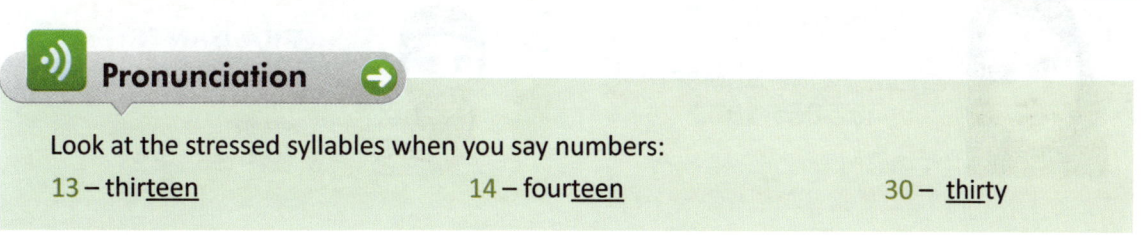

Pronunciation

Look at the stressed syllables when you say numbers:

13 – thir<u>teen</u>   14 – four<u>teen</u>   30 – <u>thir</u>ty

2. Let's play bingo. Choose nine numbers from 1 to 30. Write the numbers on the bingo card below. Write the numbers with a pencil.

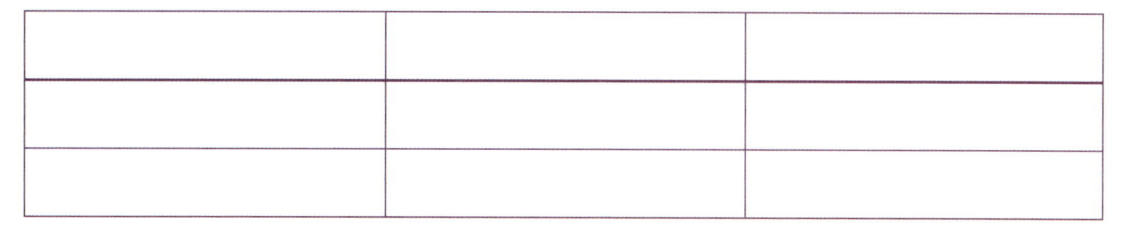

3. Now listen to your teacher and cross out (x) the numbers you hear.

4. Listen to Ricardo. Complete the information. (TRACK 17)

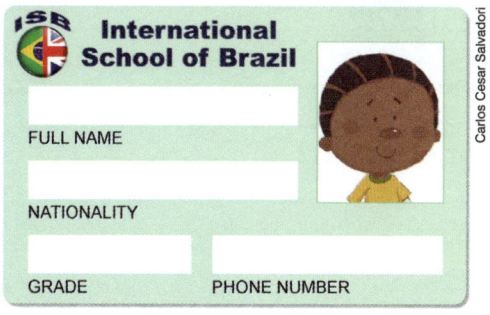

ISB — International School of Brazil

FULL NAME

NATIONALITY

GRADE   PHONE NUMBER

Carlos Cesar Salvadori

✏️ Write

1. Look at the students' cards below. Who are these people? Where are they from?

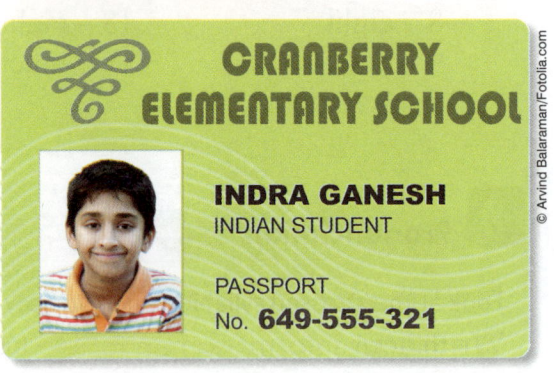

Washington Elementary School
HELEN GOMES
ID 342511720

MADISON ELEMENTARY SCHOOL
CHANG — FAMILY NAME
LIÚ — FIRST NAME
CHINA — ORIGIN 2013

WEST ELEMENTARY SCHOOL
KELLY SCOTT
TELEPHONE NUMBER: 492-856-1673
E-mail: kscott@wes.com

CRANBERRY ELEMENTARY SCHOOL
INDRA GANESH
INDIAN STUDENT
PASSPORT No. 649-555-321

💬 Remember that:

kskott@wes.com
We say
kskott **at** wes **dot** com

2. Now answer the questions about the students' card.

   a) Who is from India? _____

   b) Who is Chinese? _____

   c) Who has an ID 342511720? _____

   d. Who has a telephone number? _____

3. Are the cards different or similar?

   _____
   _____

4. And you? Do you have a similar student's card?
   _____

5. Answer the questions below.

   a) What's your full name?
   _____

   b) Where are you from?
   _____

   c) What's your school's name?
   _____

   d) What's your telephone number?
   _____

   e) What's your e-mail?
   _____

6. Now it's your turn. Make you own student's card.
   Write your information on it.

Click

<www.stb.com.br/>. Acesso em: 13 jun. 2011.

Site para pessoas que querem estudar, viajar ou trabalhar em outro país. Se você tiver o cartão desta agência de intercâmbio, você pode conseguir descontos quando viaja ou trabalha fora do seu país de origem.

Let's have fun!

let's play!

Find the hidden objects in the picture.

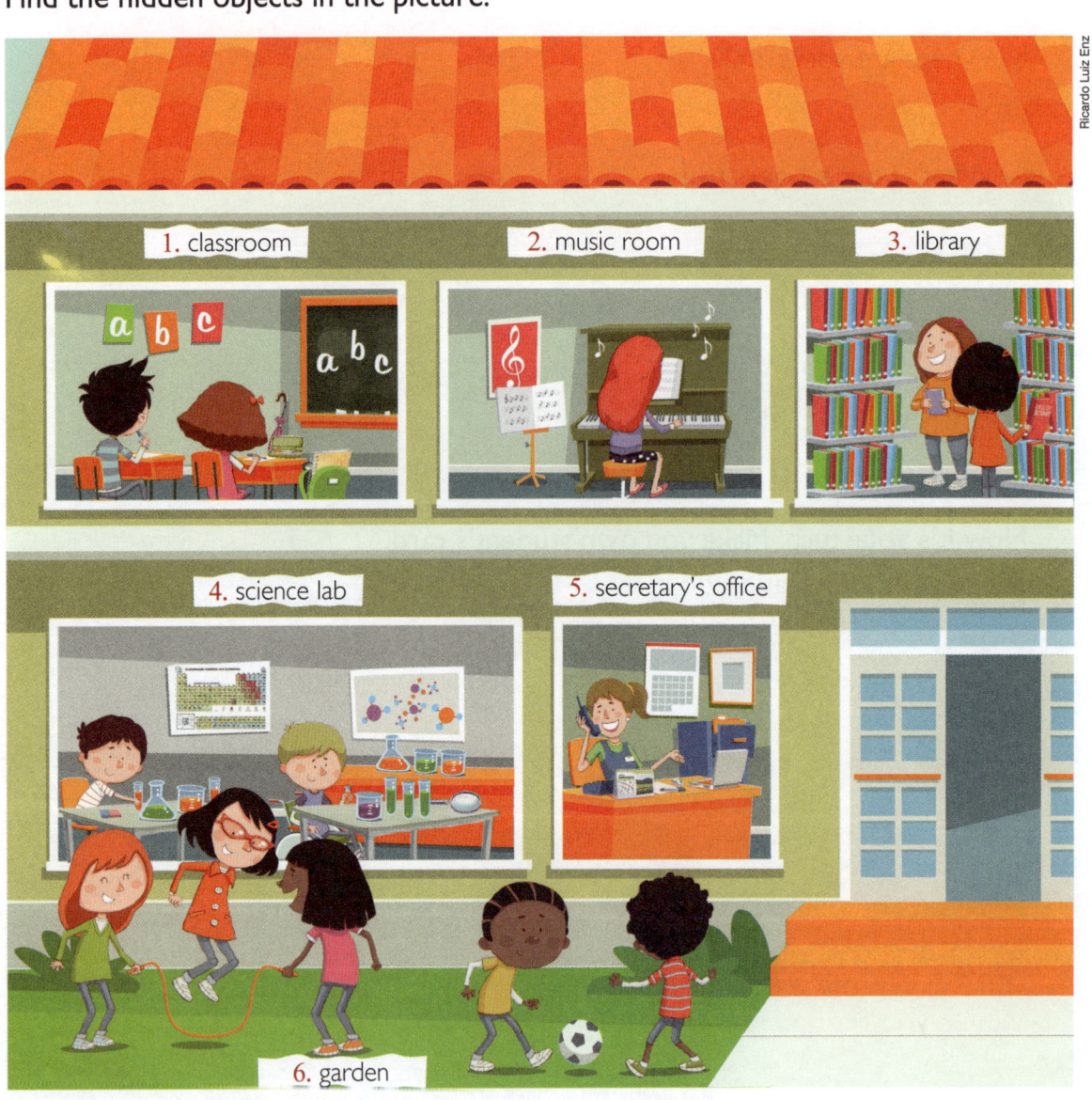

1. classroom
2. music room
3. library
4. science lab
5. secretary's office
6. garden

Where is it?

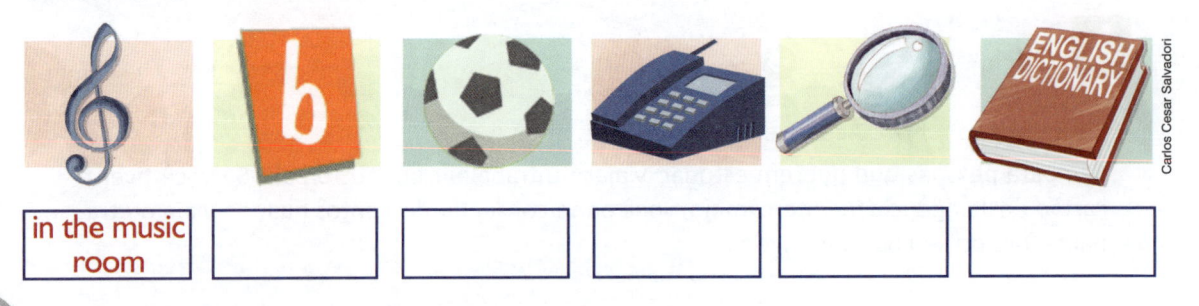

in the music room					

Exercise the mind →

1. Look at the website below. It's about a different school. It's a school which travels around the world: Roadschooling.

TO THE INTERNATIONAL TRAVELING BOARDING SCHOOL

Think Global School is a private non-profit high school that travels the world, allowing students the chance to study in three new international cities each academic year.

Exploring new cities, experiencing new cultures and learning from one another empowers our students as they develop the capacity, understanding and passion needed to make a profound difference in the world.

Read more at: <http://thinkglobalschool.org/>. Access on: Jun. 14th, 2011.

2. If you take a look at this school's website and check the curriculum, it says that there are seven school subjects (disciplines):
Anthropology, Creative arts, Global studies (history, geography and cultural studies), mathematics, sciences, world languages (at the moment of the access to the site, they teach Spanish and Mandarin and world literature).

3. Do high schools in Brazil have these disciplines in their curriculum?

4. What do you think is necessary to study in a school like this?

5. Are the students from this school coming to Brazil?
Would you like to study there?

Click →

<http://veja.abril.com.br/infograficos/think-global-school/>. Acesso em: 14 jun. 2011.
Leia um artigo sobre como essa escola para alunos do ensino médio combina desenvolvimento acadêmico e experiências globalizadas.

UNIT 4

MY FAMILY

- Present (to be) – Describing family relationships and professions

WARM-UP: What is a royal family?
Where is this royal family from?

Read

1. Look at Prince Charles' family tree.

The British Royal Family

- George Windsor VI
- The Queen Marguerite
- Prince Andreas of Greece
- Princess Alice of Battenberg
- HM The Queen Elizabeth II
- HRH Duke of Edinburgh
- HRH The Prince of Wales
- Princess Anne Elizabeth Alice Louise
- Andrew Albert Windsor
- Edward Anthony Windsor

2. Read the people's names on the family tree.
- Do you know who they are?
- Would you like to belong to a royal family?

3. Study the illustration below.

GABRIELA'S FAMILY TREE

Grandparents
- Grandfather: Paulo Melo
- Grandmother: Tânia Melo

Grandparents
- Grandfather: Rafael Silva
- Grandmother: Sara Aguiar Silva

Parents
- Uncle: Julio Melo
- Mother: Patrícia Melo Silva
- Father: Manoel Silva
- Aunt: Lúcia Silva

Gabriela is Pedro's sister.

- Gabriela Silva
- Brother: Pedro Silva

4. Listen and repeat. TRACK 18

5. Now answer the questions:

a) What's this? _____

b) What kind of information does the illustration contain?

_____

c) Look at the family tree again. Can you guess the meaning of the words in the family tree?

_____

Click

<www.royal.gov.uk>. Acesso em: 15 jun. 2011. *Site* oficial da família real britânica.

Listen

1. Look at Gabriela's family again. What is she talking about?

Remember that:

Personal Pronouns	Possessive Adjectives
I	MY
YOU	YOUR
HE	HIS
SHE	HER
IT	ITS

2. Listen and repeat.

SOME PROFESSIONS

A TEACHER

A STUDENT

AN ARCHITECT

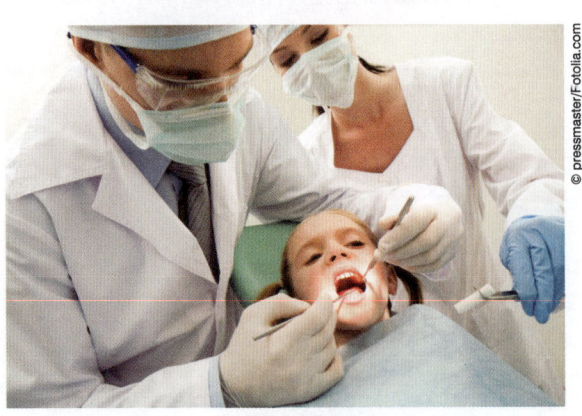

A DENTIST

Speak

1. Read the dialogue.

Laura is talking to David about her family.

Laura: Look, David! This is my family.

David: Who's this?

Laura: This is my father. He's Juan Pablo.

David: And who's this?

Laura: This is my mother. She's Consuelo. I love my parents!

2. Now it's your turn. Provide a picture of your family. Practice the dialogue with your friends in the classroom. Change roles.

3. Talk about the pictures.

Follow the model in letter **a**.

a)  He's Mr. Silva. He's a math teacher.

b)

c)

d)

e)

f)

41

Grammar points

1. Look and read.

   > She is Cate. Her name is Cate.

   > He is David. His name is David.

   > It is a dog. Its name is Lucky.

2. Now study the chart with the verb **to be** in the affirmative form.

Full Forms	Short Forms
I am Sarah.	I'm Sarah.
You are Lyndon.	You're Lyndon.
She is Mrs. Costa.	She's Mrs. Costa.
He is Mr. McCarthy.	He's Mr. McCarthy.
It is Lucky.	It's Lucky.

3. Now complete the dialogues.

   > Who's he?
   > He's Ricardo.

   > Who's she?

   > I'm Kazuki.

   > She's Miss Santos. She's the secretary.

42

> **Remember that:**
> - We use **who** when we ask about people. Who is he? He's David Parker.
> - Short form of who is = who's
> - We can also use the demonstrative pronouns with **who**:
>   Who's this? He's Lyndon.
>   Who's that? She's Cate.

Vocabulary

MORE PROFESSIONS

1. Listen and repeat.

A DOCTOR   A BUSINESSWOMAN   AN ENGINEER   A SOCCER PLAYER

2. Gabriela has a scrapbook. Look at the dialogue below and practice.

a) Father / math teacher

b) Mother / dentist

Mrs. Costa: Who's this?
Gabriela: This is my father. He's a math teacher.

43

Write

1. This is Laura's family tree. Where's she in the family tree? Circle her name.

```
        Gonzalo ─── Julieta
              │
     ┌────────┴────────┐
Juan Pablo ─ Consuelo   Esteban ─ Cecilia
     │                      │
 ┌───┼───┐              ┌───┴───┐
Javier Angel Laura   Constanza Carmen
```

Laura is talking to Lyndon about her family tree.

2. Look at the family again and complete her answers.

a) Lyndon: Who is Gonzalo?
   Laura: **He's my grandfather.**

b) Lyndon: Who is Esteban?
   Laura: _____

c) Lyndon: Who is Cecilia?
   Laura: _____

d) Lyndon: Who is Constanza?
   Laura: _____

3. Are the sentences True (T) or False (F)?

a) (**T**) Gonzalo and Julieta are Laura's grandparents.

b) (   ) Carmem is Laura's sister.

c) (   ) Angel is Constanza's brother.

d) (   ) Juan Pablo is Javier's father.

e) (   ) Juan Pablo and Consuelo are Laura's parents.

44

4. Now let's talk about your family. Write numbers in each line.

Sisters	( ) yes	( ) no	If yes, how many? _____
Brothers	( ) yes	( ) no	If yes, how many? _____
Grandfathers	( ) yes	( ) no	If yes, how many? _____
Grandmothers	( ) yes	( ) no	If yes, how many? _____
Uncles	( ) yes	( ) no	If yes, how many? _____
Aunts	( ) yes	( ) no	If yes, how many? _____

5. Now it's your turn. Look at Laura's family tree again and draw your family tree. Write people's names. Describe the relationships.

Click

<www.makemyfamilytree.com>. Acesso em: 15 jun. 2011.

Site que mostra como fazer uma árvore genealógica e também uma lista com árvores genealógicas de celebridades.

Don't miss!

GUIBERT, François de. **Pais separados**: e eu, como fico? São Paulo: Escala, 2007. Livro que fala da necessidade de adaptação a novas configurações familiares.

Let's have fun!

charades who's who?

1. Gabriela has some charades to solve about the members of her family. Help her answer the questions. Look at her family tree on page 39.

   a) He's the father of her brother.
      Manoel Silva.

   b) She's the sister of her father.
      _____

   c) She's the mother of her father.
      _____

   d) He's the father of her mother.
      _____

   e) He's the brother of her mother.
      _____

   f) She's the mother of Gabriela's brother.
      _____

2. Now based on the questions in exercise 1 create some charades for the people in your family. Share them with your friends.

Exercise the mind

- Are you a digital speaker?
- Do you think your parents can understand the way you get in contact with your friends?
- Did your parents communicate with their friends the way you do today?
- Talk about the story with your friends.

Exchanging ideas

- In your opinion, is there a limit to be connected to the Internet?
- What do you use the internet for?
- Do you think you're safe on the Internet?

Review 2: UNIT 3/4

1. Read and write.

   a)

   International School of Brazil
   NAME: LAURA FERNANDES
   CITY: BUENOS AIRES
   COUNTRY: ARGENTINA
   GRADE: 6th
   E-MAIL: laura@isb.com.br

   Miss Santos: Hello, what's your full name?

   Laura: _____

   Miss Santos: _____

   Laura: I'm from Buenos Aires, Argentina.

   Miss Santos: What's your e-mail?

   Laura: _____

   Miss Santos: Here's your student card.

   Laura: _____

   Miss Santos: You're welcome.

2. Look at this school's floor plan.

   - Computer lab
   - Science lab
   - Classroom
   - Library
   - Teachers' room
   - Music room
   - Secretary's office
   - Cafeteria
   - Art room

3. Now answer the questions.

   a) Where's the cafeteria?

   Possible answers: It's next to the art room.
   It's between the secretary's office and the art room.

48

b) Where's the art room?

_____

c. Where's the library?

_____

d) Where's the music room?

_____

e) Where's the science lab?

_____

4. Circle the word that doesn't belong.

   a) eraser – pencil – (brother) – umbrella

   b) seven – eleven – pen – twenty

   c) backpack – brother – aunt – grandparents

   d) teacher – tablet – architect – doctor

5. Unscramble the words related to professions.

   a) R-E-E-E-N-I-N-G = **engineer**

   b) T-I-N-S-E-T-D = _____

   c) O-I-N-N-B-M-W-U-A-S-E-S-S = _____

   d) R-L-A-P-Y-E = _____

   e) S-T-D-T-N-E-U = _____

6. Look at the family tree and complete the sentences.

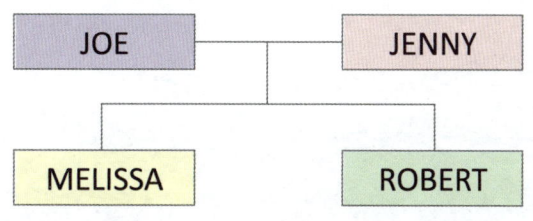

   JOE — JENNY

   MELISSA   ROBERT

   a) Joe is Melissa's **father**.

   b) Jenny is Robert's _____.

   c) Melissa is Robert's _____.

   d) Robert is Melissa's _____.

UNIT 5

LET'S EAT!

- Numbers from 40 to 100 – Describing food and drink

WARM-UP: What do you have for breakfast?
Where do you generally have lunch?
Do you like fast food?

Read

1. Look at the picture. Read the text quickly. What kind of text is it? What words do you know?

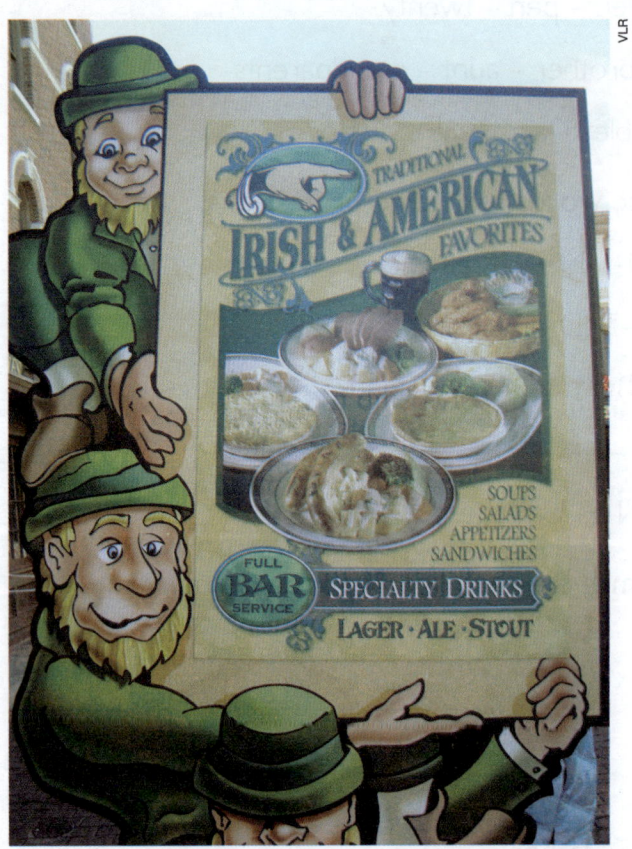

2. Discuss with your classmates. What are the key words in the text above?

3. Where can we find similar texts?

4. What kind of food do they serve at this restaurant?

5. Now look at the restaurant's menu.

SANDWICHES

Tipperary Corned Beef Sandwich
Fresh baked pretzel roll piled with warm corned beef topped with sauteed onions and Swiss cheese, garnished with lettuce, tomato and pickle. Served with wedge fries $10.99

Dublin Chicken Sandwich
Marinated grilled chicken breast topped with aged cheddar cheese and apple-smoked bacon on a toasted bun, garnished with lettuce, tomato and pickle. Served with wedge fries $10.99

Grand Ole Burger
Finnegan's big juicy burger is served on a toasted bun with your choice of Cheddar, Swiss or American cheese, garnished with lettuce, tomato and pickle spear. Served wtih wedge fries. $9.99
Make it deluxe with bacon, onions and mushrooms $1.59
Low carb version: served without the bun and with a side of broccoli

Gardenburger
Vegetarians love this all vegetable patty on a toasted bun garnished with lettuce, sliced tomato and pickle spear. Served with a medley of fresh fruits $9.79

Fried Cod Fish Sandwich
Ale battered fried cod fish served on a toasted bun with lettuce, tomato, pickle and a hearty side of tartar sauce. Served with wedge fries $10.99

Shamrock Steak Sandwich
Perfectly grilled tips of beef with peppers and onions served on a toasted baguette and wedge fries $11.99
Smother your sandwich in Provolone, Swiss, American or Cheddar cheese for only $.79

6. What kind of food is there on the menu?

_____

7. What kind of sandwiches are there on the menu?

_____
_____

8. What other information can you see on the menu?

_____

👍 Don't miss! ➡

WENDEL, Fernanda. **Seu corpo**: como cuidar dele? São Paulo: Ática, 2010.
Dicas que ensinam o adolescente a fazer suas escolhas baseadas em conceitos nutricionais valiosos.

Listen

At the cafeteria

1. Gabriela, Ricardo and Kazuki are at the school's cafeteria. It's break time. Listen to the dialogue and look at the pictures.

   TRACK 22

2. The pictures in exercise 1 are not in the correct order. Listen to the text again and number the pictures according to the events in the story. Number 1 is done for you.

3. Choose the correct alternative according to the story.

   The report card belongs to:
   a) ( ) Gabriela
   b) ( ) Kazuki
   c) ( ) Ricardo

   Who is not hungry? Who is not thirsty?
   a) ( ) Gabriela
   b) ( ) Kazuki
   c) ( ) Ricardo

   Where are the students?
   a) ( ) At school.
   b) ( ) At home.
   c) ( ) In a restaurant.

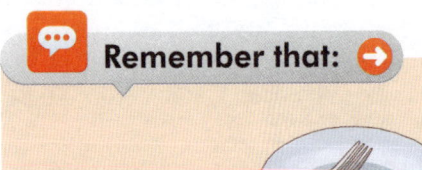

Remember that:

I'm hungry.

I'm thirsty.

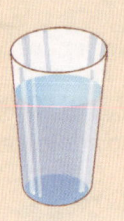

Speak

1. Read, listen and repeat the numbers from 40 to 100. TRACK 23

40 – forty	70 – seventy
50 – fifty	80 – eighty
60 – sixty	90 – ninety

100 – a hundred *or* one hundred

101 – a hundred and one *or* one hundred and one

2. Look at the pictures.

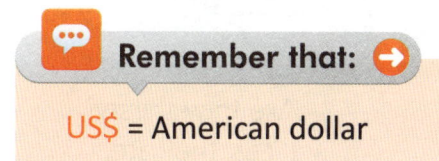

AMERICAN INTERNATIONAL SCHOOL: SNACKS OF THE MONTH

a) A ham and cheese sandwich + a bottle of orange juice = **US$ 6.75**

b) Wholemeal cookies and chocolate = **US$ 7.90**

c) A frozen yogurt and an apple pie = **US$ 8.69**

Carlos Cesar Salvadori

Remember that:

US$ = American dollar

Pronunciation

Pay attention to the **"ch"** sound in **ch**eese, sandwi**ch** and **ch**ocolate.

3. Read the dialogue between the clerk and the student about the snacks at the American International School.

   Clerk: Hello, what would you like?

   Student: A ham and cheese sandwich, please.

   Clerk: Here you are. Anything else? A drink?

   Student: Yes, a bottle of orange juice, please. How much are the sandwich and the juice?

   Clerk: They're six dollars and seventy-five cents.

   Student: Here is six dollars and seventy-five cents. Thanks.

   Clerk: You're welcome.

4. Now practice the dialogue with a classmate. Replace the underlined words. Change roles.

Remember that:

How much is / are...? = prices
How much is the orange juice? (US$ 2.00) It's two dollars.
How much are the sandwiches? (R$ 5,00) They're five reais.

Grammar points

1. Look and read.

Are you ok?
No, we are not.

Are you hungry?
No, we aren't.

Are they thirsty?
Yes, they are.

2. Now look at the chart with the verb **to be** in the interrogative, affirmative and negative forms. Complete the chart.

Interrogative	Affirmative	Negative
Am I...?	I am = I'm	I am not = I'm not
_____ you...?	You are = _____	You're not = You aren't
Is he...?	_____ = He's	He's not = He isn't
Is she...?	She is = She's	She's not = _____
_____ it...?	It is = _____	_____ = It isn't
Are we...?	_____ = We're	We're not = _____
Are you...?	You are = You're	You're not = You aren't
_____ they...?	_____ = They're	_____ = They aren't

3. Complete. Use the **personal pronouns** and the corresponding affirmative short forms of the verbs **to be**.

Hi, My name's Laura. **I'm** from Buenos Aires. Buenos Aires is the capital of Argentina. _____'s a very nice city in South America. My mother's name is Consuelo. _____ an engineer. My father isn't an engineer. _____'s a doctor. They're from Argentina, too. These are my brothers, Javier and Angel. _____'re Argentinean, too. We're a beautiful family!

Vocabulary

1. Study the menu. Listen and repeat.

BREAKFAST

coffee — milk — bread — cheese — ham — orange juice

LUNCH

salad — french fries — rice and beans — vegetables — meat — chicken

DINNER

soup — pizza — pasta — grilled fish — hot dog

DESSERTS

pie — cup cake — fruit

DRINKS

tea — water — soda

2. These are some things you can eat in a coffee shop. What about you? What do you have for:

a) Breakfast: _____

b) Lunch: _____

c) Dinner: _____

3. And what do you have at school?

_____

✏️ **Write** ➡️

1. Look at the menu. Read the information on it.

ROSE PARK – FAMILY RESTAURANT
195 INTERNATIONAL DRIVE, ORLANDO, FL (407) 276-4168

"WE DELIVER" – MENU

APPETIZERS		MAIN COURSES	
TOMATO	US$ 4.97	ROAST CHICKEN	US$ 10.85
CHICKEN WINGS	US$ 7.16	STEAK	US$ 15.93
GARLIC BREAD	US$ 2.23	PASTA	US$ 12.15
ONION RINGS	US$ 6.00	FRIED FISH	US$ 24.00

SALADS		DESSERTS	
CAESAR SALAD	US$ 3.00	ICE CREAM	US$ 1.70
CHEF'S SALAD	US$ 3.50	PUDDING	US$ 2.90
GREEN SALAD	US$ 2.80	APPLE PIE	US$ 1.80
		JELLY	US$ 0.90

DRINKS	
SODA	US$ 2.00
COFFEE	US$ 2.50
WATER	US$ 2.80
JUICES	US$ 3.20
GREEN TEA	US$ 1.15
LEMONADE	US$ 1.80

ALL THE MAIN COURSES ARE SERVED WITH RICE, VEGETABLES, AND MASHED POTATOES.

2. You're going to make a menu. Read the instructions below.
Some hints on how to make your menu.

1. You'll need menus from different places.

2. Examine the menus and the descriptions of foods.

3. Look at the colors, pictures and the words used in the menus.

4. Think about what makes the foods appealing. So provide beautiful pictures for your menu.

5. Now you're ready. Design your own menu.

6. Keep in mind the foods that the restaurant will specialize in.

7. If you don't have any pictures, draw the food and write descriptions about them.

3. Now it's your turn. In your notebook make your own menu.

Let's have fun!

food riddles for teens

Read and answer. Use the pictures to help you.

1. What are two things you cannot have for breakfast? __Lunch and dinner_____.

2. I am round and red. Some people think I'm a vegetable, but I'm not. I'm a fruit. People like to use me in salads. _____

3. I am white. You can drink me. _____

4. I am yellow and long. I am a fruit. Monkeys eat me. _____

5. I am green. When you cut me and open me I'm red. I am a summertime fruit. _____

6. I am green. I am a vegetable. I am like a tree. _____

7. I am orange. My top is green. I am a vegetable. _____

8. I am blue and round. I'm an American fruit. I am little. I'm not big. _____

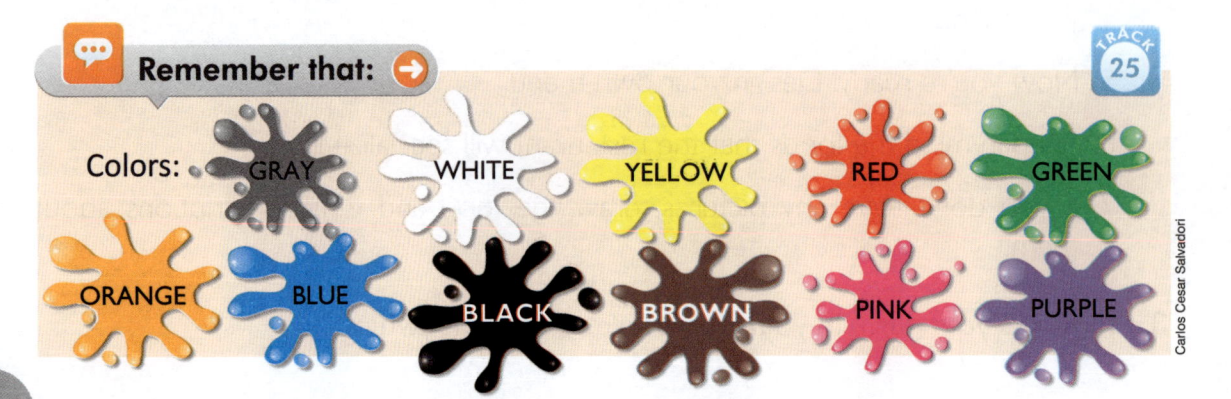

Remember that:

Colors: GRAY WHITE YELLOW RED GREEN
ORANGE BLUE BLACK BROWN PINK PURPLE

Exercise the mind

MIND MAP – FAST FOOD FACTS

FAST FOOD FACTS

- Fast food is generally cheap. They're often made with cheaper ingredients.
- Fast food refers to food that can be prepared and served very fast.
- Teens love fast food because they have busy lives. They want to eat fast food.
- Fast food is usually high in fat, calories, cholesterol and sodium.
- Many health problems may appear if you eat too much fast food: high blood pressure, heart disease and obesity.
- Teens also love junk food. This kind of food is bad for your health.

Exchanging ideas

- Most teens like fast food. Are you one of them?
- Do you eat healthy food? If yes, what do you eat?
- Think about a healthy food mind map. What kind of facts will you include on it?
- Exchange the mind maps in class.

Click

<http://alimentacao.terra.com.br/noticias/para-sua-idade-9/fast-food-saudavel-163>. Acesso em: 22 jun. 2011.
Fast food saudável: faça escolhas boas para o seu organismo. Artigo sobre algumas dicas para se alimentar melhor.

<www.ehow.com/facts_4841111_healthy-foods-teenagers.html>. Acesso em: 22 jun. 2011.
Comidas saudáveis para adolescentes. Algumas dicas sobre que tipo de comida os adolescentes devem comer.

UNIT 6

HOW IS THE WEATHER?

• Describe the weather – Describing clothing

WARM-UP: Do you check the weather forecast everyday?
How is the weather in your city today?

Read

1. Look at the weather forecast for Florida for January 10th. Where does this text come from?

CELSIUS AND FAHRENHEIT SCALES

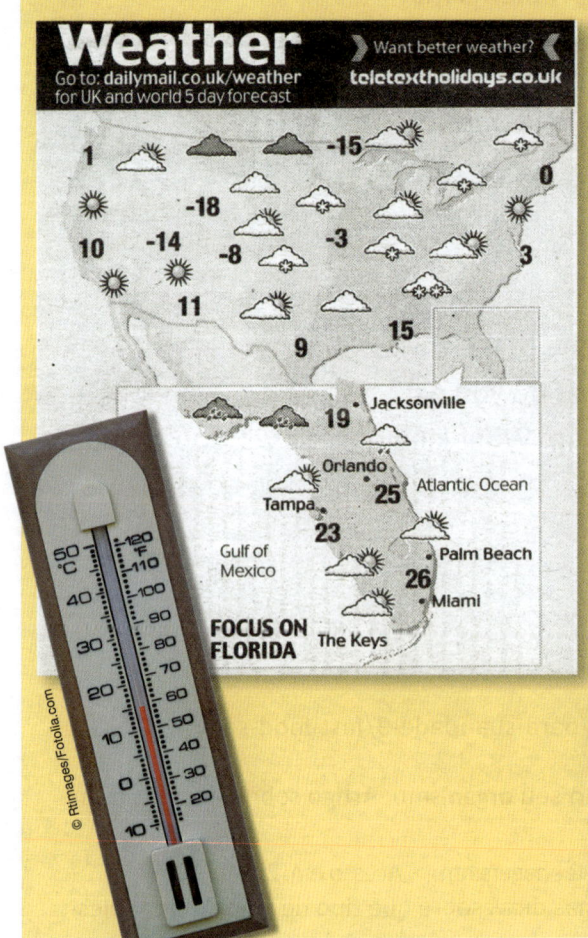

Weather
Go to: dailymail.co.uk/weather for UK and world 5 day forecast
Want better weather? teletextholidays.co.uk

FOCUS ON FLORIDA

From coast to coast, across America today

Florida will have sunny spells in the south, but cloudier in the north with rain. The Appalachians and the southeast will be cloudy with outbreaks of rain, sleet or snow. The Great Lakes and Midwest states will have sunny spells. Varying amounts of cloud for the Pacific Northwest and the Intermountain West. The Great Plains and Mississippi will be cloudy with snow. Elsewhere, sunshine.

And back in Britain today

LONDON/SOUTH EAST: Increasingly cloudy and windy with rain expected by evening. Strong winds. Max 9c (48f).
MIDLANDS: Cloudy and windy with rain spreading eastwards. Fresh winds. Max 8c (46f).
WALES: Wet with outbreaks of rain, some heavy. Fresh southwest winds. Max 9c (48f).
NORTH: A cloudy, wet and breezy day with rain and sleet or snow on high ground. Brisk winds. Max 7c (45f).
SCOTLAND: Cloudy with rain, sleet and snow. Gentle to moderate winds. Max 6c (43f).
IRELAND: A dull day with outbreaks of rain. Gentle to moderate winds. Max 9c (48f).
UK OUTLOOK TOMORROW: Fine, with just a few showers in western Scotland. Rain later in Northern Ireland.

5 day city forecast

	Tue	Wed	Thu	Fri	Sat
London	8c	13c	13c	11c	12c
Plymouth	8c	11c	12c	10c	11c
Cardiff	8c	12c	12c	11c	11c
B'ham	6c	12c	12c	11c	11c
M'chester	6c	11c	11c	10c	11c
Newcastle	4c	11c	9c	10c	10c
Glasgow	5c	9c	9c	9c	10c
Aberdeen	4c	7c	6c	8c	8c
Belfast	5c	10c	10c	9c	9c

From Daily Mail, Monday January 10th, 2011.

Learn how to convert temperatures in English.

- FROM CELSIUS TO FAHRENHEIT
    1. Determine the temperature in Celsius;
    2. Multiply the temperature by 1.8;
    3. Add 32 to the result;
    4. The final answer is the temperature in Fahrenheit.

    Ex: 20 °C
    20 x 1.8 = 36 + 32 = 68 °F

- FROM FAHRENHEIT TO CELSIUS
    1. Determine the temperature in Fahrenheit;
    2. Subtract 32;
    3. Divide the answer by 1.8;
    4. The final answer is the temperature in Celsius.

    Ex: 68 °F
    68 − 32 = 36 : 1.8 = 20 °C

Exchanging ideas

- What's the temperature in Miami in degrees Fahrenheit?
- What's the temperature in your city in degrees Celsius?
- What scale is used in Brazil to measure the temperature?

2. Look at the weather forecast on page 60 again. Answer the questions.

   a) In the 5 day city forecast section, what's the temperature in London on Thursday?
      ___13 °C___ .

   b) What's the temperature in Cardiff on Friday? _____

   c) What's the temperature in Glasgow on Wednesday? _____

Why learn?

Cardiff is the capital of Wales.

Glasgow is the largest city in Scotland.

3. Look at the weather symbols below.

sunny

windy

rainy

snowy

cloudy

foggy

4. Look at the weather forecast again on page 60. Look at the USA map. Answer the questions.

a) How is the weather in Orlando? It's rainy.

b) How is the weather in Palm Beach? _____

Don't miss!

ESCOTT, John. **Hannah and the Hurricane**. Penguin Readers Longman.

História de Hannah que leva pessoas para passear todos os dias. Até que um dia chega um furacão.

Listen

1. Listen to the weather forecast. Check the best responses.

a) What's the name of the weather man?
   ( ) Nic Farmer.
   ( ) Dick Farmer.
   ( ) Nic Gardner.

b) The weather forecast report is for:
   ( ) Sunday.
   ( ) Monday.
   ( ) Friday.

c) Where is the weather man?
   ( ) At school.
   ( ) At home.
   ( ) At the airport.

d) What is the temperature?
   ( ) 27 °C.
   ( ) 27 °F.
   ( ) 37 °C.

2. In the previous exercise, the weather man says it's the first day of summer in Brazil. Look and check the seasons in Brazil in the Southern Hemisphere:

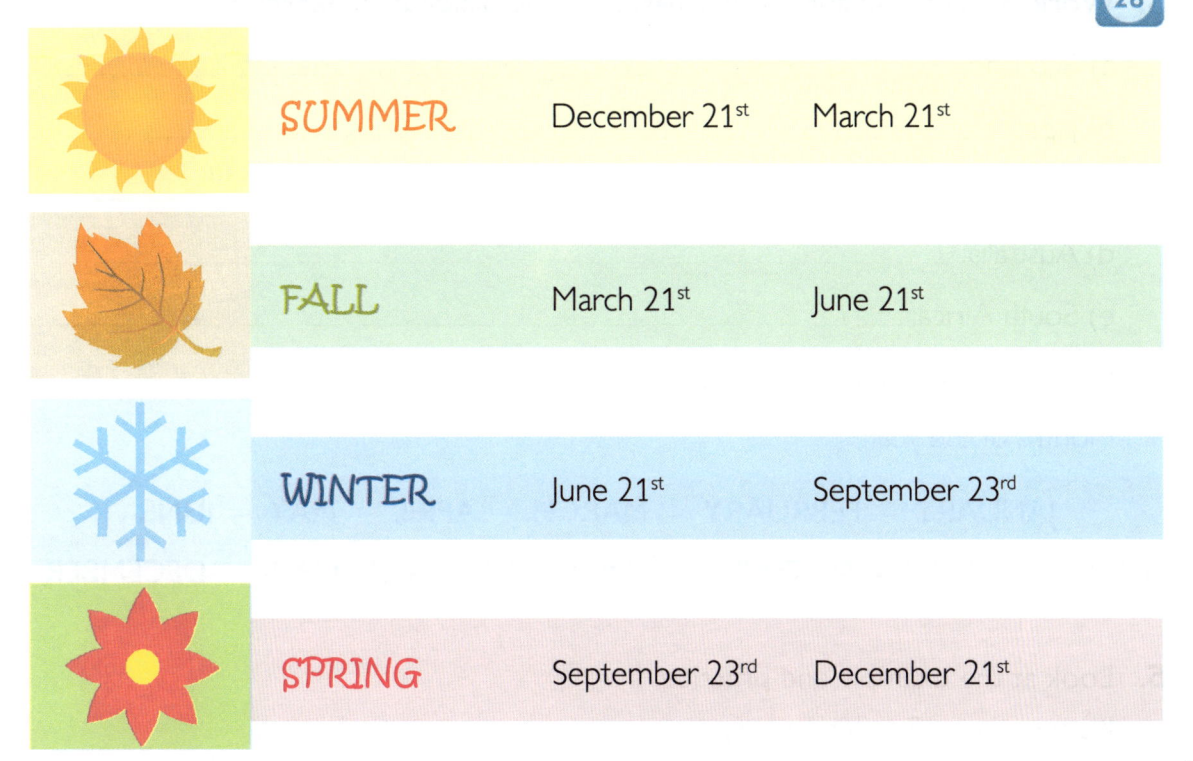

☀	SUMMER	December 21st	March 21st
🍂	FALL	March 21st	June 21st
❄	WINTER	June 21st	September 23rd
🌺	SPRING	September 23rd	December 21st

63

Speak

1. Look at the map and the weather conditions.

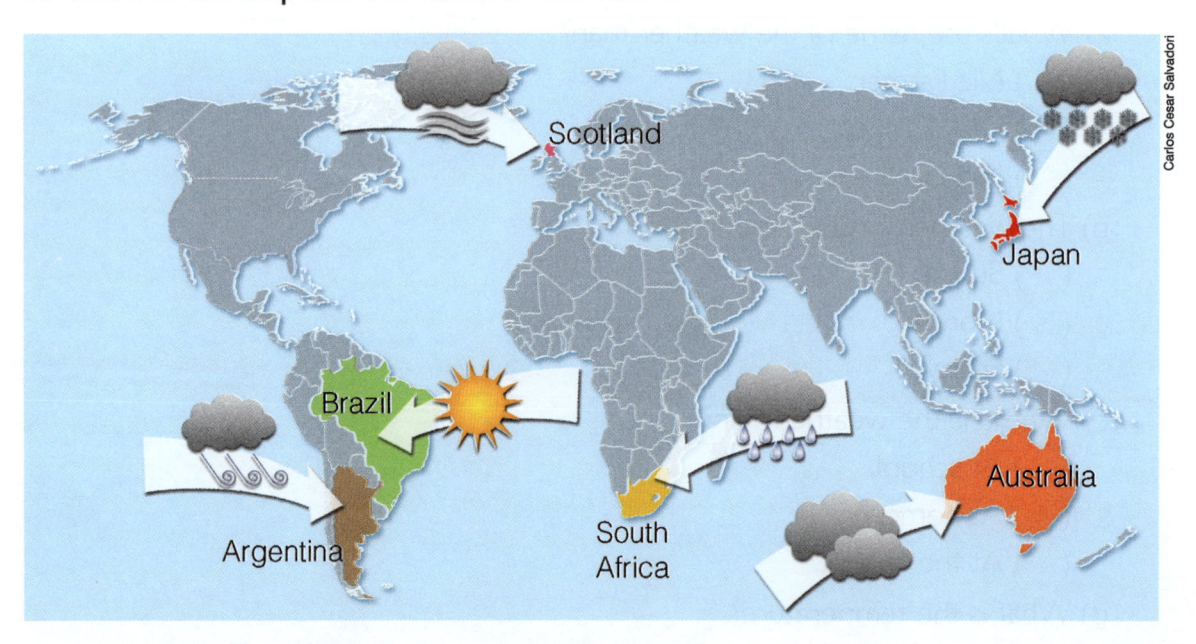

2. Now look at the example. Practice.

- Brazil
  Student A: How is the weather in Brazil?
  Student B: It's sunny.

3. Work in pairs. Ask and answer based on the dialogue in exercise 2.

a) Scotland: _____

b) Japan: _____

c) Argentina: _____

d) Australia: _____

e) South Africa: _____

4. Listen and repeat the months of the year. TRACK 29

Months of the year.

> JANUARY – FEBRUARY – MARCH – APRIL – MAY – JUNE
> JULY – AUGUST – SEPTEMBER – OCTOBER – NOVEMBER – DECEMBER

5. Look at the example and practice.

It's summer in Brazil in January.

Grammar points

1. Look at the picture.

WEDNESDAY, MAY 10th

2. Now answer the questions about the picture.

a) How is the weather in the picture? _____

b) Who's in the picture? _____

c) What's the date today? _____

d) What's the store's address? _____

3. Check what you need to write and say dates and addresses.

DATES
Today is March 23rd, 2012.
My birthday is **on** October 24th.

ADDRESSES
The store is **at** 137 Main Street.
The store is **on** Main Street.

ORDINAL NUMBERS

1st	first	11th	eleventh	21st	twenty-first
2nd	second	12th	twelfth	22nd	twenty-second
3rd	third	13th	thirteenth	23rd	twenty-third
4th	fourth	14th	fourteenth	24th	twenty-fourth
5th	fifth	15th	fifteenth	25th	twenty-fifth
6th	sixth	16th	sixteenth	26th	twenty-sixth
7th	seventh	17th	seventeenth	27th	twenty-seventh
8th	eighth	18th	eighteenth	28th	twenty-eighth
9th	ninth	19th	nineteenth	29th	twenty-ninth
10th	tenth	20th	twentieth	30th	thirtieth

Vocabulary

1. Look, listen and repeat.

	Hot Weather	Cold Weather
David	Shorts	Jacket
Sarah	Dress	Coat
Ricardo	T-Shirt	Jeans
Gabriela and Laura	Skirt	Sweater
Cate	Blouse	Sweatpants
Kazuki and David	Cap	A sweatshirt
Lyndon	Sneakers	Socks

Remember that:

Shorts, jeans, socks, sneakers and sweatpants are in the plural form.
My socks are white.

2. Write sentences according to the table on the previous page. Use the genitive and the possessive cases correspondingly.

a) David's shorts are yellow.   His jacket is gray.

b) _____   _____

c) _____   _____

d) _____   _____

e) _____   _____

f) _____   _____

g) _____   _____

💬 Remember that:

Genitive case: David's shorts are yellow.

Possessive case: His shorts are yellow.

🔊 Pronunciation

Attention for the **"sh"** sound in **sh**orts and T-**sh**irt.

✏️ Write

1. Check the weather symbols on page 62. Write the adjectives you know. Check the new symbols and adjectives.

Sunny

Stormy   Dry

2. Look at the thermometers and complete.

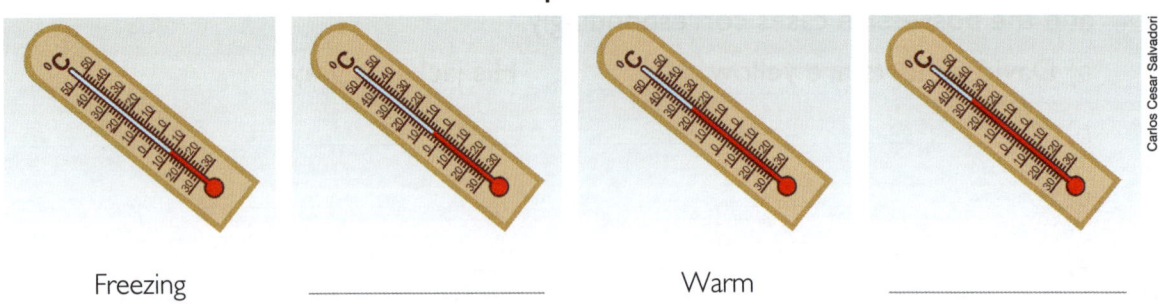

Freezing _____ Warm _____

3. Draw the weather symbols in the windows below to indicate different kinds of weather. Write sentences about the weather. There's one example for you.

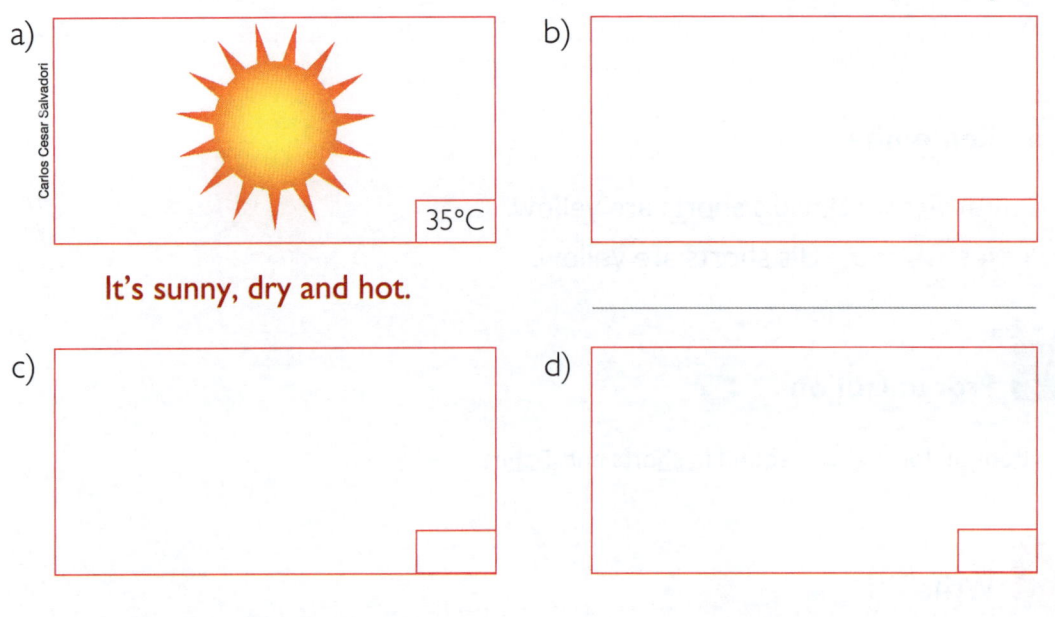

a) 35°C

It's sunny, dry and hot.

b) _____

c) _____

d) _____

4. Read Gabriela's paragraph about summer in Brazil. She used some weather symbols in it.

Summertime is generally hot in Brazil. In January and February it's 🌧. It's not dry. I like it when the weather is ☀. I drink water and juice. I wear shorts, dresses and T-shirts. In the morning sometimes the weather is ☁.

At night the temperature is warm, but it's rarely cold. Summer is my favorite season.

💬 **Remember that:** ➡

Rarely, generally and sometimes are adverbs of frequency.

5. Now copy the paragraph here. Change the weather symbols into words.
Summertime is generally hot in Brazil. (…)

_____
_____
_____
_____
_____

6. Now it's your turn. Write a similar paragraph with the weather symbols on the previous page. Choose another season. Exchange paragraphs with your classmates.

Let's have fun!

1. Talk to a classmate about the differences in the two pictures.

picture 1

picture 2

2. Write sentences about the pictures.

In picture one...	In picture two.
The weather is sunny.	The weather is cloudy.

> **Exercise the mind** →

traditional clothing around the world

1. Men in Scotland sometimes wear a kilt on special occasions. It is a short wool skirt held up with a wide black belt. Men say that they're warm and comfortable.

2. Read the information about a typical Scotsman.

   Bow Tie: it must match with the white shirt.

   Sporran: the leather pouch must be worn approximately three or four fingers below the belt.

   Kilt Pin: must be fastened on the right side of the kilt.

   Kilt: should be adjusted to the waist and must not go below the knee. The pleats are to be worn in the back.

   Stockings: they must be folded and be two or three fingers below the knee.

   Ribbons: must be worn externally along the side of the legs, with 1/3 covered by the fold of the stockings.

   © Yuri Arcurs/Fotolia.com

3. Would you like to wear this traditional clothing in Brazil?

   _____

4. Which of the clothing items above would you not like to wear?

   _____

5. What are some traditional clothing items in the region where you live?

   _____

6. Work in pairs. In your notebook, write a description of a traditional clothing worn in Brazil.

   _____

> **Click** →

<www.ehow.com/about_5377218_traditional-clothes-brazilians-wear.html>.
Acesso em: 13 jul. 2011.

Quais são algumas roupas tradicionais usadas por brasileiros? Artigo que fala como os brasileiros também usam roupas tradicionais em ocasiões e celebrações especiais.

Review 3: UNIT 5/6

1. Look at the pictures below. Copy the sentences from the box in to the corresponding balloons.

> We're from Brazil. — They're from Brazil. —
> You're from Japan. — ~~You're my parents.~~

a)

b)

c) You're my parents.

d)

2. Write the words.

		S	A	L	A	D			
			R		I				
C	H	I	C	K	E	N			
			I		E	*	C	R	E	A	M
	F	R	E	N	C	*	F	R	I	E	S

3. Look at the pictures and complete with **this**, **that**, **these** or **those**.

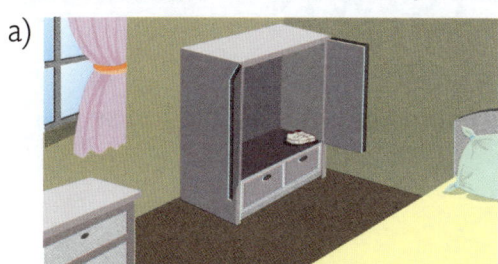

a) **Those** are Cate's sneakers.

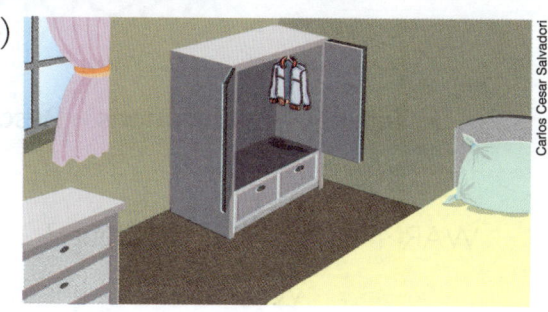

b) _____ is Lyndon's jacket.

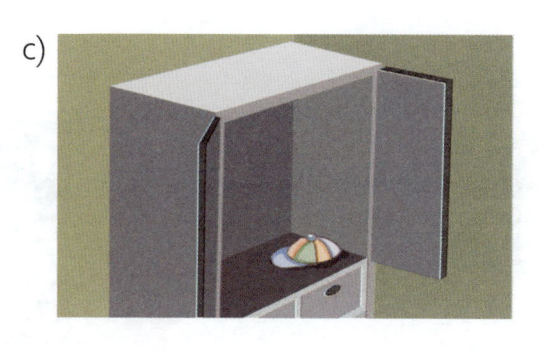

c) _____ is Kazuki's cap.

d) _____ are David's shorts.

4. Write sentences. Use the possessive adjectives. Follow the model.

a) My book and your book are next to our desk.
   Our books are next to our desks.

b) Gabriela's dress is red and white.

   _____

c) Kazuki's socks are blue.

   _____

d) Lyndon's and Laura's coats are black.

   _____

5. Write the ordinal numbers in full.

5th = **fifth**

12th = _____

17th = _____

20th = _____

29th = _____

32nd = _____

33rd = _____

21st = _____

UNIT 7

AROUND TOWN

- Talking about locations – Describing rooms and things in a house

WARM-UP: What is a museum?

What are museums for?

Do you like to visit museums?

Read

1. Read the information about the Musée Océanographique Monaco. What type of text is it? What images can you see?

2. Look back at the text. What words do you know?

3. Where is this museum? Would you like to visit this museum?

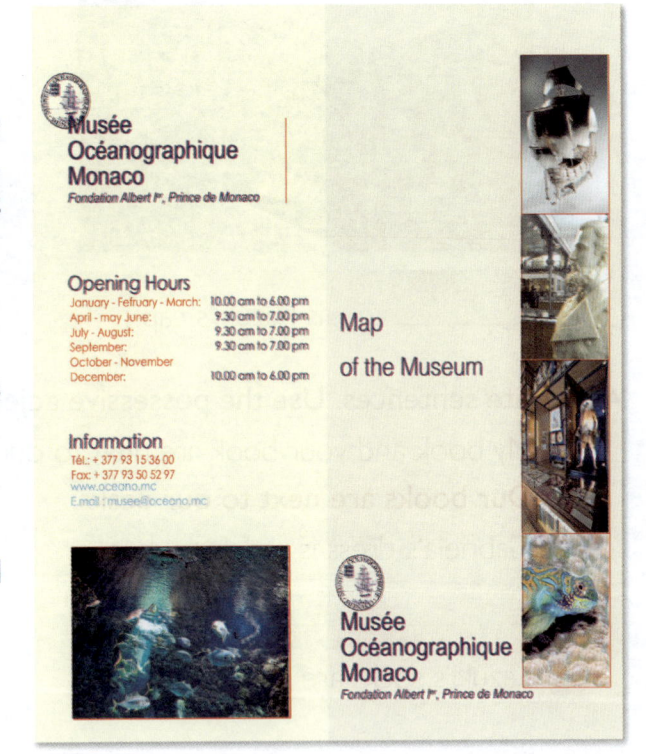

Exchanging ideas

- Are there oceanographic museums in Brazil?

Click

<www.museu.furg.br/museu_oceanografico.html>. Acesso em: 13 jul. 2011.
Site of Museu Oceanográfico "Prof. Eliezer de Carvalho Rios" in Rio Grande, RS.

74

4. Read the text again and check if the sentences are True (T) or False (F) or it doesn't say (X).

   a) The museum is located in Monaco. **T**

   b) The museum's website is www.oceano.mc. _____

   c) If you want more information, you can send an e-mail to musee@oceano.mc. _____

   d) The museum opens in the morning everyday. _____

   e) The museum opens from January to December. _____

5. Take a look at other interesting places to visit in a city.

   a) a shopping mall

   b) a park

   c) a zoo

   d) a movie theater

   e) a theater

   f) a public library

6. Listen and repeat. (TRACK 32)

Exchanging ideas

- Name some other places people can enjoy when they visit a city.

Click

<http://travel.nationalgeographic.com/travel/countries/brazil-guide>. Acesso em: 13 jul. 2011.
Website com fotos de lugares no Brasil.

75

Listen

1. Kazuki, Gabriela and Ricardo are downtown. Listen and practice.

Kazuki: I'm hungry. Let's go to the Internet Café.
Gabriela: That's a good idea. But where is it?
Ricardo: It's on Second Street.
Gabriela: Is it across from the bank?
Kazuki: No, it isn't. It's next to the bank.

Pronunciation

'S': Street, store and station are different from the supermarket.

2. Now look at the map. What public places can you see?

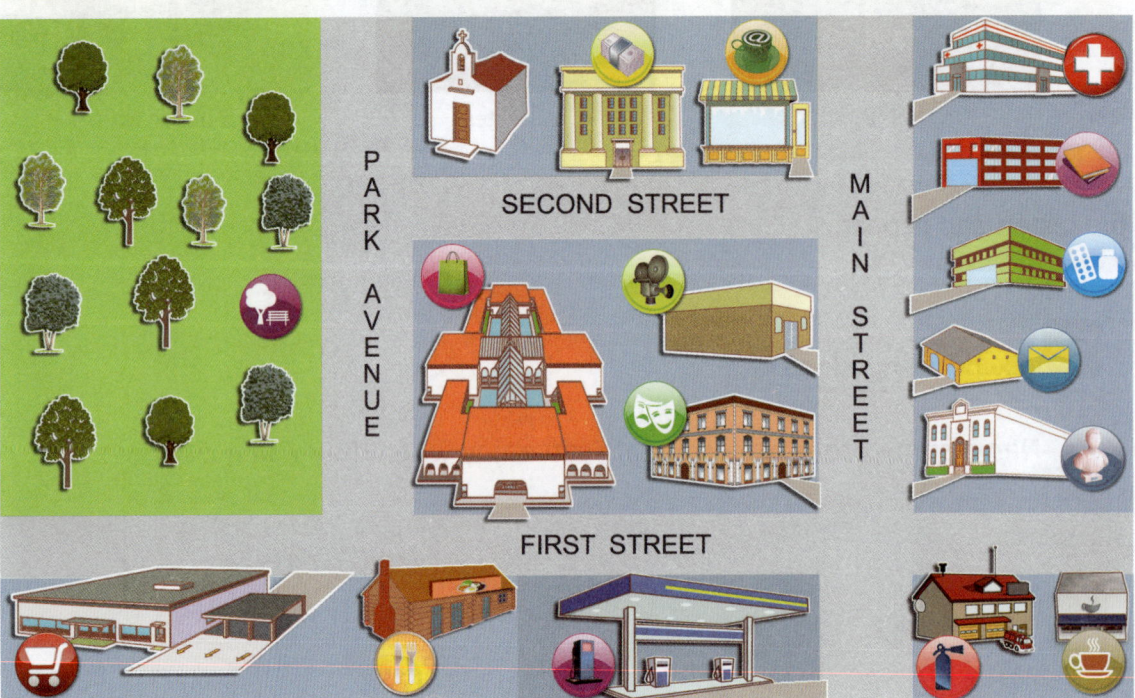

Shopping Mall · Supermarket · Fire Station · Coffee Shop · Museum · Hospital · Internet Café · Post Office
Restaurant · Gas Station · Drugstore · Movie Theater · Bookstore · Park · Bank · Theater

PARK AVENUE · SECOND STREET · MAIN STREET · FIRST STREET

3. Now listen and point to the place in the map.

> **Why learn?**
>
> It's important to know how to label these public places when you visit a foreign city. This kind of vocabulary is a must for you.

Speak

1. Look at the pictures. Read the dialogues.

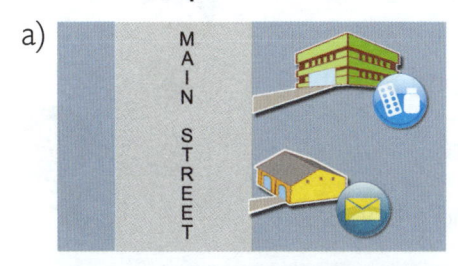

   a) Gabriela: Where's the drugstore?
   Kazuki: It's _____ Main Street, _____ the post office.

   b) Gabriela: Where's the museum?
   Kazuki: It's on Main Street _____ the theater.

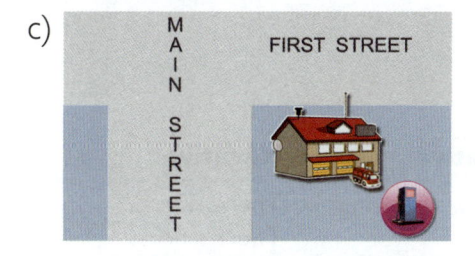

   c) Gabriela: Where's the fire station?
   Kazuki: It's _____ Main Street and First Street.

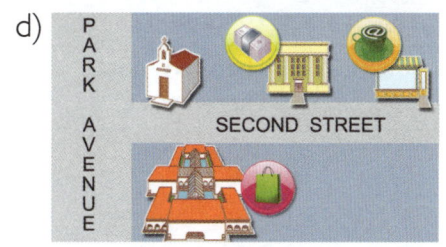

   d) Gabriela: Where's the bank?
   Kazuki: It's _____ Second Street _____ the shopping mall.

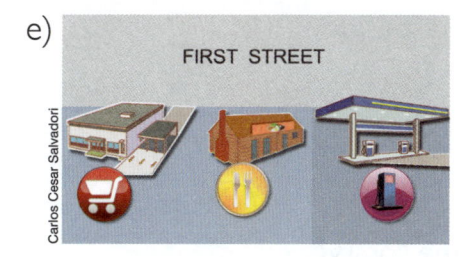

   e) Gabriela: Where's the restaurant?
   Kazuki: It's _____ First Street _____ the supermarket and the gas station.

2. Now in pairs practice the dialogue. Include new places from the previous map.

Grammar points

1. Look at the map on Page 76. Now listen to the dialogue between Gabriela, Kazuki and Ricardo.

TRACK 35

Gabriela: Is there a post office on Main Street?

Kazuki: Yes, there is.

Ricardo: Is there a bank on First Street?

Kazuki: No, there isn't. There's a bank on Second Street.

Gabriela: Are there any stores on Main Street?

Kazuki: Yes, there are. There is a drugstore and a bookstore.

Ricardo: Are there any restaurants on Park Avenue?

Kazuki: No, there aren't. There is a restaurant and a coffee shop on First Street.

Carlos Cesar Salvadori

Remember that:

- **There to be (Present)** = Existence

	Interrogative	Affirmative	Negative
Singular	Is there...?	There is... There's...	There is not... There's not... There isn't...
Plural	Are there...?	There are...	There are not... There aren't...

2. Underline the correct alternatives.

a) Is there / <u>Are there</u> any students at school?

b) There isn't / aren't a bookstore next to my house.

c) There is / are some banks in my city.

d) Is there / Are there a hospital across from the library?

e) There isn't / aren't any drugstores downtown.

Vocabulary

1. Rooms in a house. Look at the picture. Listen to the parts of the house.

bedroom · bathroom · bedroom

living room · dining room · kitchen · garage

2. Listen to the new vocabulary.

a — kitchen: a microwave, a refrigerator, a stove

b — dining room: a table, a chair

c — living room: a TV set, a sofa

d — bedroom: a wardrobe, a desk, a bed

e — bathroom: a shower, a sink, a toilet

3. Ask and answer the questions about the picture in exercise 2. Use **there + to be**.

Student 1: Is there a table in the kitchen?
Student 2: Yes, there is.

Write

1. Look at these events.

Saturday evening	Friday afternoon	Tuesday night	Sunday morning
Soccer game City Stadium 6:00 p.m.	Shopping mall Birthday party 3:30 p.m.	Music concert Globe Theater 8:30 p.m.	Extra sessions for children Cinejoy Movie Theater 10:00 a.m.

2. Now answer the questions:

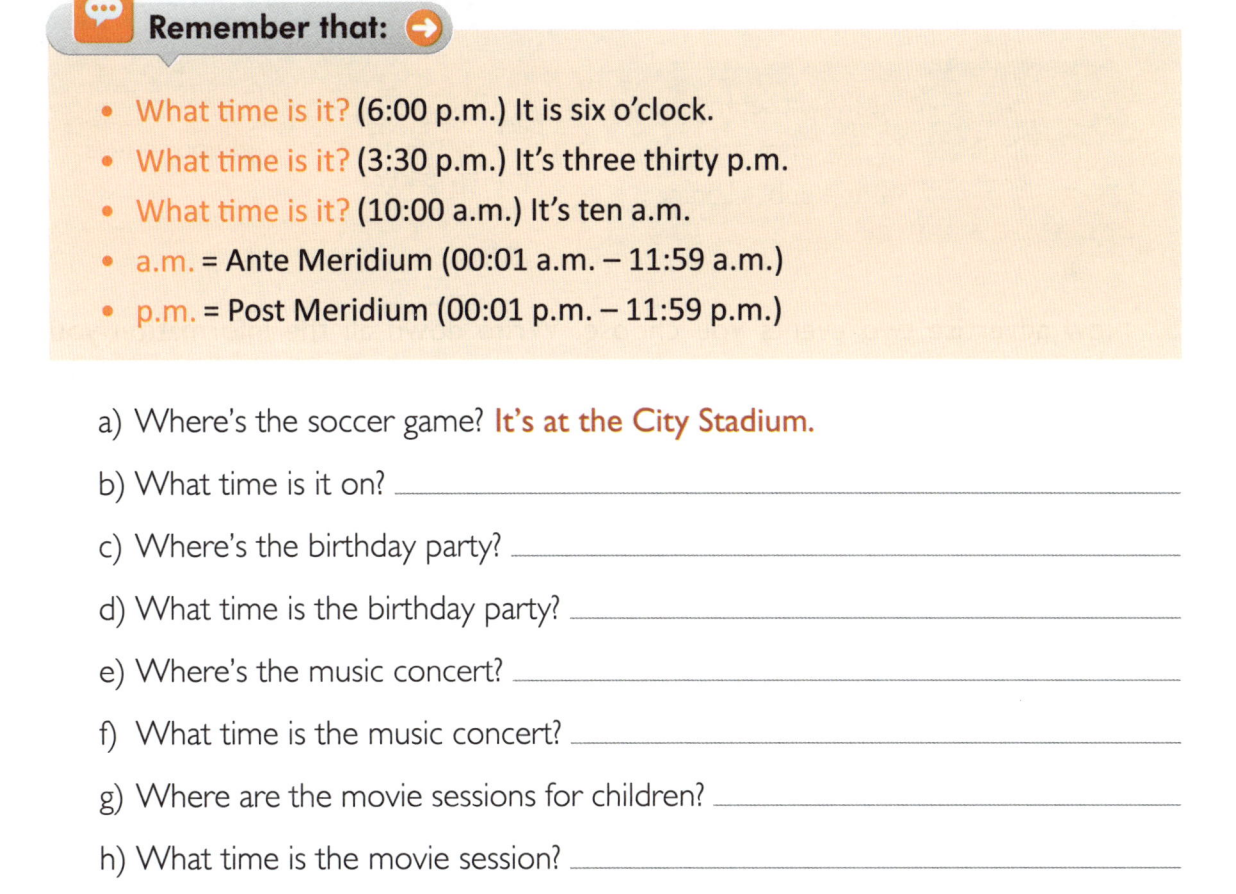

> **Remember that:**
> - What time is it? (6:00 p.m.) It is six o'clock.
> - What time is it? (3:30 p.m.) It's three thirty p.m.
> - What time is it? (10:00 a.m.) It's ten a.m.
> - a.m. = Ante Meridium (00:01 a.m. – 11:59 a.m.)
> - p.m. = Post Meridium (00:01 p.m. – 11:59 p.m.)

a) Where's the soccer game? **It's at the City Stadium.**

b) What time is it on? _____

c) Where's the birthday party? _____

d) What time is the birthday party? _____

e) Where's the music concert? _____

f) What time is the music concert? _____

g) Where are the movie sessions for children? _____

h) What time is the movie session? _____

> **Remember that:**
>
> We use the preposition **at** before hours.

3. Write sentences about the events. Use <u>There is</u>.

a) There's a soccer game on Saturday at 6:00 p. m.

b) _____

c) _____

d) _____

4. Now it's your turn.

Think about two events in different places. Here are some suggestions.

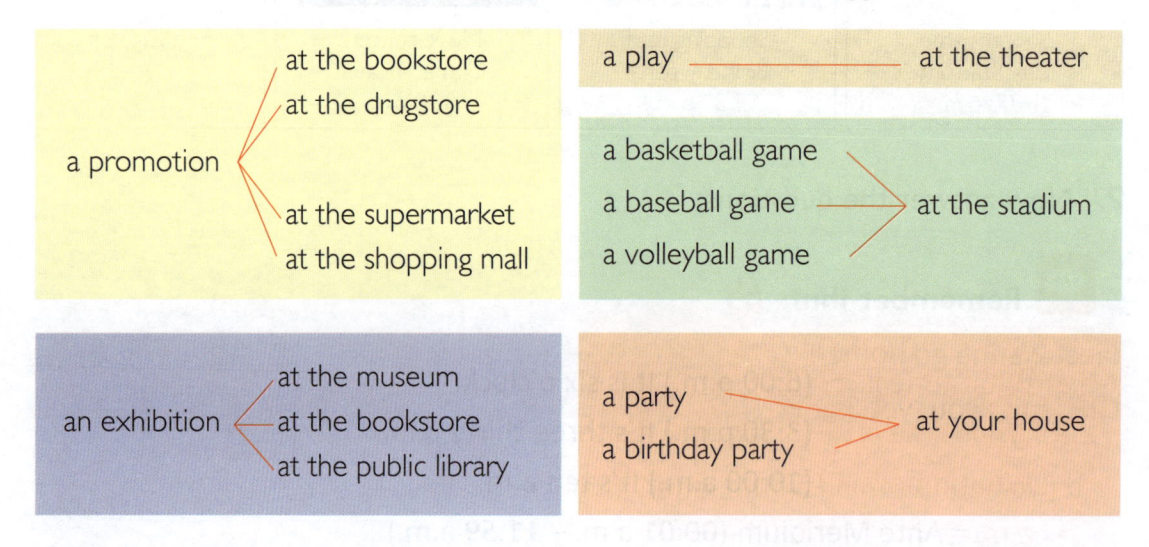

a promotion	at the bookstore at the drugstore at the supermarket at the shopping mall

a play	at the theater

a basketball game a baseball game a volleyball game	at the stadium

an exhibition	at the museum at the bookstore at the public library

a party a birthday party	at your house

5. Now advertise two events you choose. Write down all the information you think might be necessary:

Let's have fun!

1. Listen to the song. Fill in the gaps.

home

Michael Bublé, David Foster, Bill Ross

Another summer day
Has come and gone away
In Paris and Rome
But I wanna go _____

Maybe surrounded by
A million people I
Still feel all alone
I just wanna go home
Oh, I miss you, you know

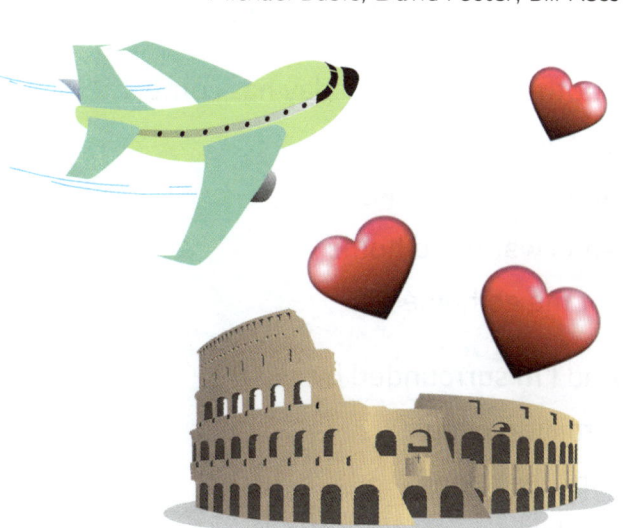

And I've been keeping all the letters that I wrote to _____
In each one a line or two
"I'm fine baby, _____?"
Well I would send them but I know that it's just not enough
My words were _____ and flat
And you deserve more than that

Another airplane
Another _____ place
I'm lucky I know
But I wanna go home
Mmmm, I've got to go home

Let me go home
I'm just too far
From _____ you are
I wanna come home

Carlos Cesar Salvadori

83

And I feel just like _____ living someone else's life
It's like I just stepped outside
When everything was going right
And I know just why you could not
Come along with me
Cause this was not your dream
But you always believed in me

Another _____ day has come
and gone away
And in Paris and Rome
And i wanna go home
Let me go home

And I'm surrounded by
A million people
I still feel alone
Oh, let me go home
Oh, I miss _____, you know

Let me go home
I've had my run
Baby, I'm done
I gotta go home

Let me go home
It will all be alright
I'll be _____ tonight
I'm coming back home

Available at: <http://letras.terra.com.br/michale-buble/128318>. Access on: October 26th, 2011.

Click

<www.youtube.com/watch?v=IbSolbmuvie>. Acesso em: 28 jun. 2011.
Você pode assistir ao vídeo desta música.

Exercise the mind

1. Look at the pictures. Where do you live?

A mobile home

An igloo

A nursing home

A house / An apartment

2. Read the quotation below. Do you agree with it? Talk to your classmates.

> "Where we love is home. Home that our feet may leave, but not our hearts."
>
> OLIVER WENDELL HOLMES, SR. "Homesick in heaven"

Exchanging ideas

- Do you like where you live?
- What do you think it'd be like to live in the houses in the pictures above?
- Discuss with your classmates different **words** that mean "home".

UNIT 8

TALENTS

- Talking about talents and skills

WARM-UP: What is a quotation?
Do you like quotations?
Can you remember a famous quotation?

Read

1. Look at the quotations. What are they about?

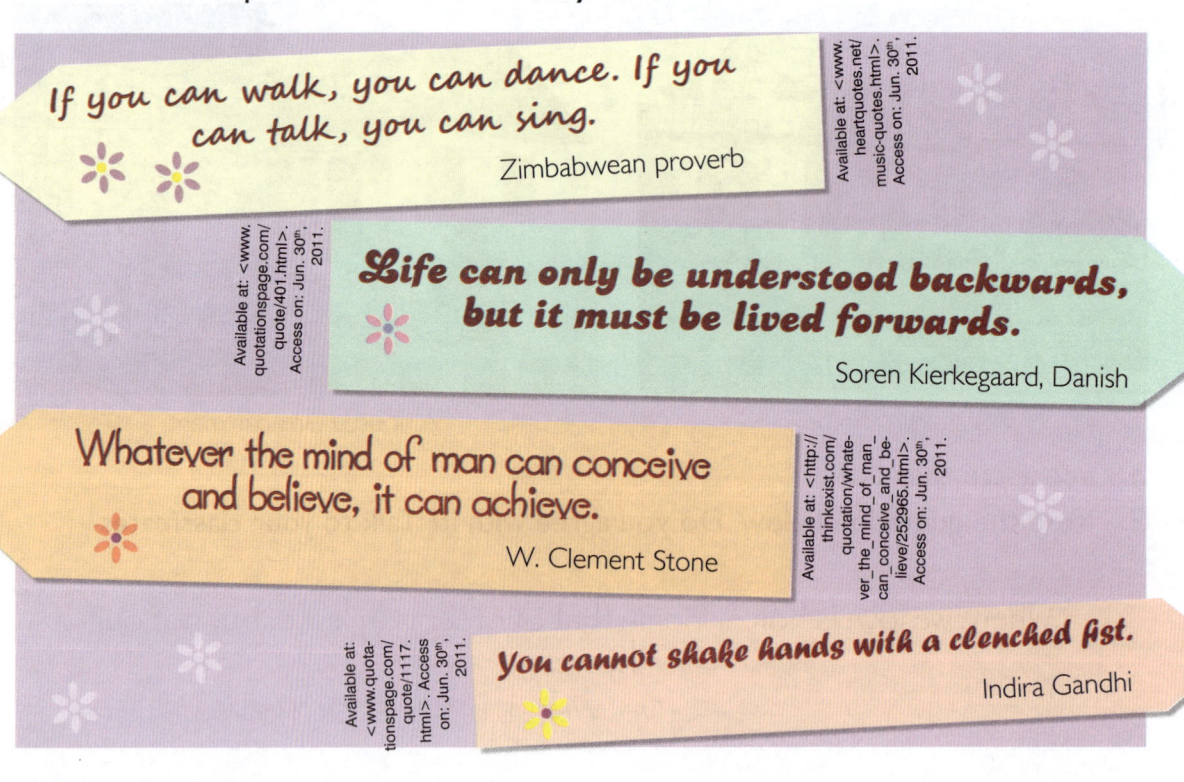

If you can walk, you can dance. If you can talk, you can sing.
Zimbabwean proverb

Available at: <www.heartquotes.net/music-quotes.html>. Access on: Jun. 30th, 2011.

Life can only be understood backwards, but it must be lived forwards.
Soren Kierkegaard, Danish

Available at: <www.quotationspage.com/quote/401.html>. Access on: Jun. 30th, 2011.

Whatever the mind of man can conceive and believe, it can achieve.
W. Clement Stone

Available at: <http://thinkexist.com/quotation/whatever_the_mind_of_man_can_conceive_and_believe/252965.html>. Access on: Jun. 30th, 2011.

You cannot shake hands with a clenched fist.
Indira Gandhi

Available at: <www.quotationspage.com/quote/1117.html>. Access on: Jun. 30th, 2011.

Click

<www.quotationspage.com/>. Acesso em: 13 jul. 2011. *Site* com citações de pessoas famosas.

<http://quotations.about.com/>. Acesso em: 13 jul. 2011. Nesse *website* você pode selecionar citações cômicas, de amizade e sobre aniversários.

2. Look at these people.

3. What can they do?

> **Exchanging ideas**
>
> - There are students who find it really hard to join in with sports and games at school.
> - There are students who use wheelchairs.
> - There are students who can't run as fast as your classmates. These people have special needs. They require assistance for disabilities.
> - What about you? Do you know any students with a disability in your school? Does anyone in your family have a disability?
> - What things are they good at? What can they do?

Listen

1. There are some activities at ISB. Look at the bulletin board.

International School of Brazil

Enroll in these extracurricular activities. Come and join us!

a) Sing and dance hip hop

b) _____

c) _____

d) _____

e) _____

f) _____

2. Now label the pictures with the words from the box. Then listen and practice.

TRACK 38

| Play the guitar – Swim – Draw and paint – |
| ~~Sing and dance hip hop~~ – Ride a horse – Speak Chinese |

3. Gabriela and Kazuki talk about the extracurricular activities.

Gabriela: Look! There are some extracurricular activities at school. Let's enter.

Kazuki: No, thanks.

Gabriela: Yes, let's. I can play the guitar but I can't ride a horse. Can you ride a horse?

Kazuki: Yes, I can.

Gabriela: Great! So let's enter, ok?

Kazuki: Ok. Let's.

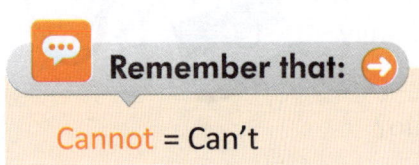

Remember that:

Cannot = Can't

Speak

1. Read the questions. Write two more questions.

   What can you do?

   a) Can you speak French?
   b) Can you skateboard?
   c) Can you play tennis?
   d) Can you ride a bicycle?
   e) _____
   f) _____

2. Now, answer the questions. Use the symbols below in the chart.

   Can you play the piano?

   - Yes, I can (✓)
   - No, I can't (✗)

	YOU		CLASSMATE 1		CLASSMATE 2	
	CAN	CAN'T	CAN	CAN'T	CAN	CAN'T
a)						
b)						
c)						
d)						
e)						
f)						

3. Now ask two classmates the questions from **a** to **f** in exercise 1.

4. Now report what you and your classmates can and can't do.

   Example: I can speak French.

   My classmate (1) _____ can / can't speak French.
   (name)

   My classmate (2) _____ can / can't speak French.
   (name)

5. Listen and check. Do they say **can** or **can't**? TRACK 39

   a) ( ) can
      ( ) can't

   b) ( ) can
      ( ) can't

   c) ( ) can
      ( ) can't

   d) ( ) can
      ( ) can't

Grammar points

1. Complete.

Can and Can't

Interrogative	Affirmative	Negative (Cannot / Can't)
Can I	I can	I _____
Can you	You _____	You can't
Can he make a sandwich?	He can sing in Portuguese.	He _____ swim 1000 meter.
Can she	She _____	She can't
_____ we	We _____	We can't
_____ they	They can	They _____

2. Look at the chart below. ✓ = Yes / X = No

	Make a cake	Play table tennis	Read Spanish	Send a text message	Ride a motorbike
Gabriela	✓	X	✓	✓	X
Lyndon	✓	✓	X	✓	X
Laura	✓	X	✓	✓	X
Cate	X	X	X	✓	X
David	X	✓	X	✓	X

3. Now answer the questions. Use short forms.

a) Can Lyndon send a text message?
   Yes, he can.

b) Can Cate read Spanish?
   _____

c) Can David play table tennis?
   _____

d) Can Laura ride a motorbike?
   _____

e) Can Gabriela make a cake?
   _____

Vocabulary

1. Look at these pets and check what they can do.

ANIMALS: What can they do?

A dog can walk on four legs.

A bird can sing.

A cat can jump.

A parrot can talk.

Fish can swim.

A rabbit can run very fast.

2. Listen and repeat.

3. What pets do they have?

a) My pet's name is Lucy. She's blue with white wings. She's nice. She can fly and sing, but she can't talk. What is she?

b) My pet's name is Felix. He's black and white. He can catch mice. He can jump. He likes milk.

91

Write

1. Look at the picture. What's happening?

2. Now listen to David talking about how to help students who use wheelchairs like him.

    TRACK 41

    a) WHEN CHATTING KEEP EYE TO EYE ON THE SAME LEVEL.

    b) TRY TO IDENTIFY A TABLE THAT IS EASILY ACCESSIBLE.

    c) CHECK IF THERE ARE NO BARRIERS WHEN CHANGING ROOMS.

    d) WE CAN HELP PEOPLE.

3. And you? Do you find it difficult to help people like David?

4. **What about you?**

Can you think about other ways to help students like David? Discuss it with your friends.

5. **Now write a poster to be hung on your school's walls.**

Things to consider when writing your poster.

- Always show respect for students who are in some way "different".
- Are there any ramps for wheelchairs in your school? Keep the focus: see your classmate, not his / her disability.
- Are there any accessible bathrooms in your school?
- Use the right words to describe their particular disabilities. Do not hurt or insult your classmates.
- Remember that all able-bodied students have a chance to be helpers.
- When the poster is ready, hang it on your school's walls.

Exchanging ideas

- Talk with your classmates about people who have overcome disabilities and even achieved greatness.
- Read this quotation from Stephen Hawking. What do you think?

" The downside of my celebrity is that I cannot go anywhere in the world without being recognized. It is not enough for me to wear dark sunglasses and a wig. The wheelchair gives me away'.

Available at: <www.goodreads.com/author/quotes/1404. Stephen_Hawking>. Access on: July 1st, 2011.

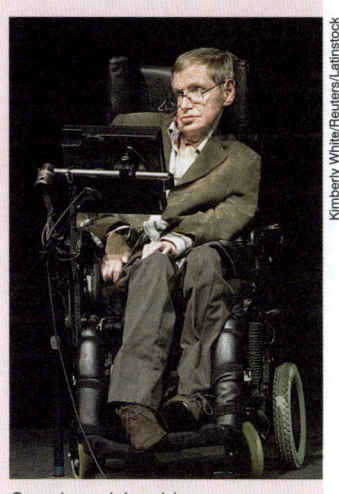

Stephen Hawking.

Click

<www.wikihow.com/enjoy-walt-Disney-world-with-a-Mobility-disability>. Acesso em: 1 jul. 2011.
Leia sobre como pessoas com necessidades especiais transitam dentro dos parques da Disney.

Let's have fun!

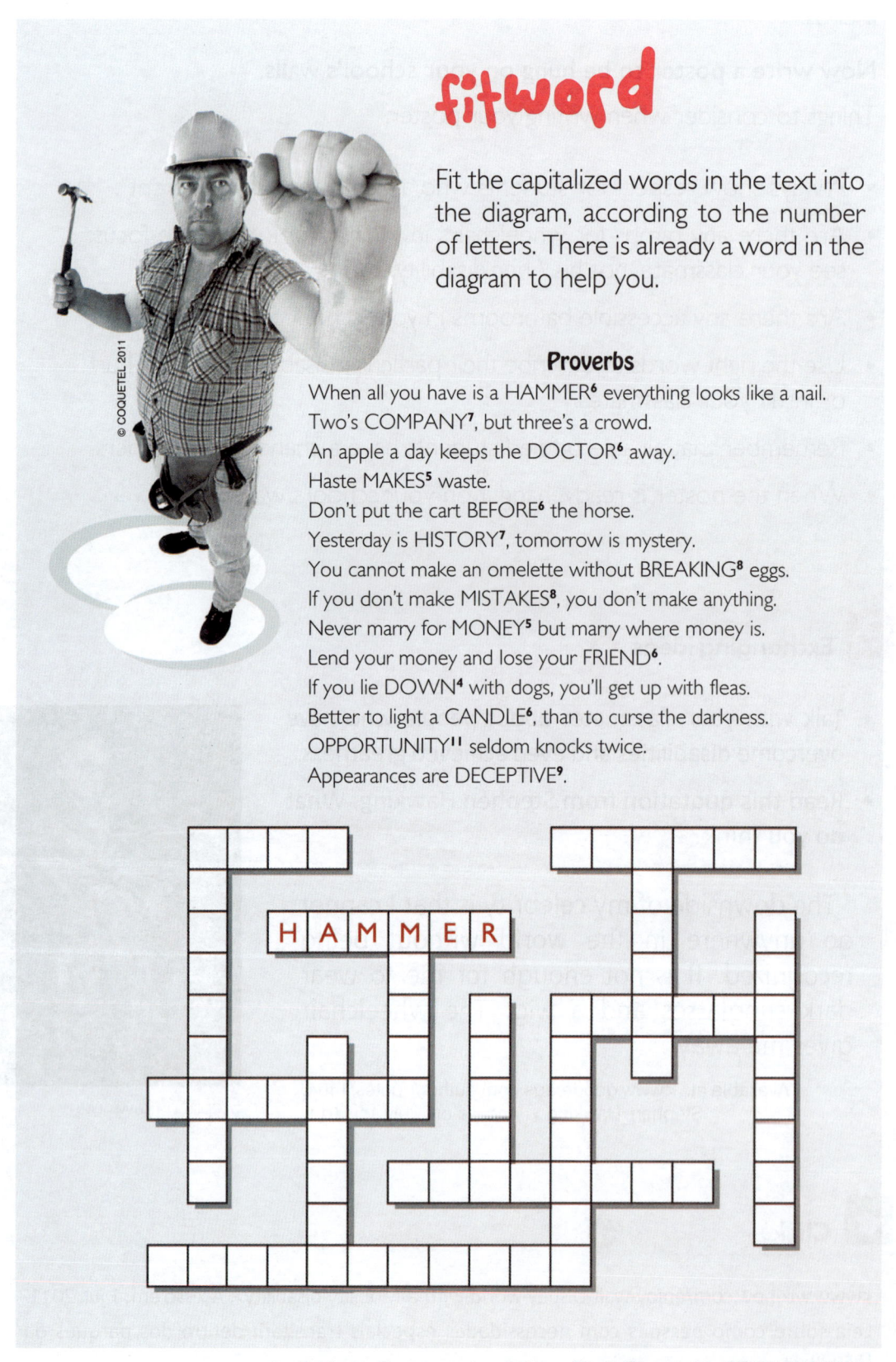

fitword

Fit the capitalized words in the text into the diagram, according to the number of letters. There is already a word in the diagram to help you.

Proverbs

When all you have is a HAMMER[6] everything looks like a nail.
Two's COMPANY[7], but three's a crowd.
An apple a day keeps the DOCTOR[6] away.
Haste MAKES[5] waste.
Don't put the cart BEFORE[6] the horse.
Yesterday is HISTORY[7], tomorrow is mystery.
You cannot make an omelette without BREAKING[8] eggs.
If you don't make MISTAKES[8], you don't make anything.
Never marry for MONEY[5] but marry where money is.
Lend your money and lose your FRIEND[6].
If you lie DOWN[4] with dogs, you'll get up with fleas.
Better to light a CANDLE[6], than to curse the darkness.
OPPORTUNITY[11] seldom knocks twice.
Appearances are DECEPTIVE[9].

Available at: Cross words n.º 64, p. 30. © Copyrights COQUETEL 2011.

Exercise the mind

PETS

1. On this page you can see parts of pets' bodies. Look at the pictures. Guess which animals they are.

2. In pairs or in groups, talk about the "for" and "against" when having pets.

For 👍	Against 👎
• Children can play with pets. • Pets are also good companions for older people. • Dogs can help visually and hearing impaired people. • Cats can kill mice, rats and other animals.	• Pets make a mess when they're walking on the street. • Pets can be dangerous. They can also hurt people. • It's expensive to have pets. • Some people can't afford pets.

3. What about you? Do you agree or disagree with the statements in the chart from exercise 2?

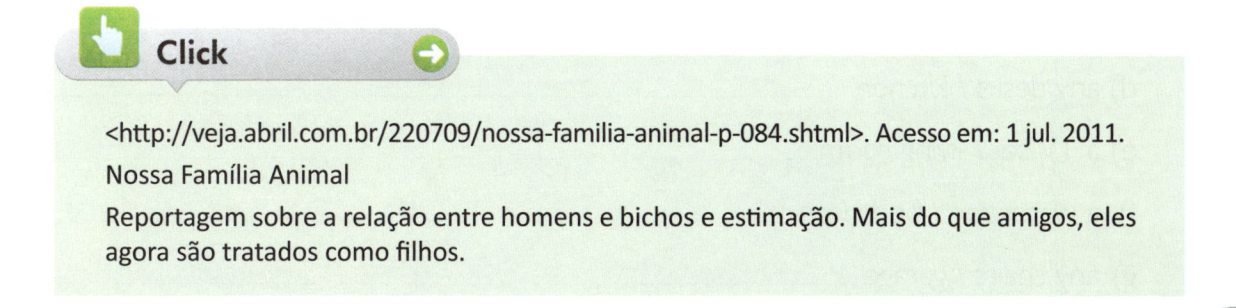

Click

<http://veja.abril.com.br/220709/nossa-familia-animal-p-084.shtml>. Acesso em: 1 jul. 2011.

Nossa Família Animal

Reportagem sobre a relação entre homens e bichos e estimação. Mais do que amigos, eles agora são tratados como filhos.

Review 4: UNIT 7/8

1. Look at this house.

2. Now write affirmative and negative sentences. Use the hints to help you use "there to be".

a) a refrigerator / kitchen

   There's a refrigerator in the kitchen.

b) some chairs / dining room. _____

c) a sofa / bathroom. _____

d) any desks / kitchen. _____

e) a TV set / living room. _____

f) a wardrobe / bedroom. _____

g) any chairs / garage _____

3. Write questions and answers.

a) Gabriela can read Spanish. ✓

   Can Gabriela read Spanish? Yes, she can.

b) Lyndon can ride a motorbike. ✗

   Can Lyndon ride a motorbike? No, he can't.

c) Lyndon and Laura can make a cake. ✓

_____

d) David can send a text message. ✓

_____

e) Gabriela and Laura can play table tennis. ✗

_____

4. Write four sentences, two affirmatives and two negatives. What can you do?

a) I can _____

b) I can _____

c) I can't _____

d) I can't _____

5. Look at the words below. Copy them in the corresponding boxes.

Spanish – blue – T-shirt – play soccer – milk – cookies – water – skirt – geography – brown – speak French – cake – dress – history – white – jump – soda – sandwich

Colors	Subjects	Abilities
	Spanish	

Clothes	Food	Drink

Workbook

Unit 1

1. It's the first day at school. Look at the pictures.

    a) [Picture: Cate and Kazuki meeting outside a school]
    - Hi! My name's Cate. What's your name?
    - Hi, Cate. I'm Kazuki.

    b) [Picture: Two girls talking]
    - Are you English, Laura?
    - No, I'm not. I'm Argentinean. I'm from Buenos Aires.

2. Who said these sentences? Write the names.

    a) What's your name? **Cate**

    b) Are you English, Laura? _____

    c) I'm Kazuki. _____

    d) No, I'm not. _____

    e) Hi, Cate. _____

    f) I'm from Buenos Aires. _____

3. Circle the correct words to complete the dialogues.

    a) What's your name?

    My (name) / country is Edward.

    b) Where are you to / from?

    I'm from Portugal.

    c) Are you from New York?

    No, I'm no / not. I'm from Atlanta, USA.

98

4. Look at the words below. Write them in the correct places to complete the dialogue.

> South Africa — from — ~~Hello~~ — you — Are — am

Lyndon: Hi, Kazuki.

Kazuki: **Hello**, Lyndon.

Lyndon: _____ you _____ Japan?

Kazuki: Yes, I _____. Where are you from?

Lyndon: I'm from _____. I'm from Cape Town.

5. Find six countries in the crossword. Then write them.

a) **Japan**   b) _____
c) _____   d) _____
e) _____   f) _____

Q	W	E	W	A	R	G	E	N	T	I	N	A	I	L
A	A	L	D	Q	D	L	R	E	Q	U	E	D	O	I
G	S	A	C	A	I	K	G	S	A	H	D	G	L	Z
J	S	G	B	U	F	J	K	D	S	R	G	L	Y	A
A	D	U	M	I	G	D	N	A	L	G	N	E	G	R
P	L	T	L	O	H	M	L	G	F	E	L	M	F	B
A	M	R	H	P	J	H	O	H	K	R	O	N	D	Q
N	N	O	E	A	K	B	U	J	L	L	U	V	F	A
Z	L	P	F	S	L	F	Y	K	Y	O	H	B	S	D
C	E	O	C	D	Ç	D	R	L	B	M	K	H	H	G
V	B	E	R	T	A	U	S	T	R	A	L	I	A	J

99

Unit 2

1. Find six school objects in the word snake. Then write the words.

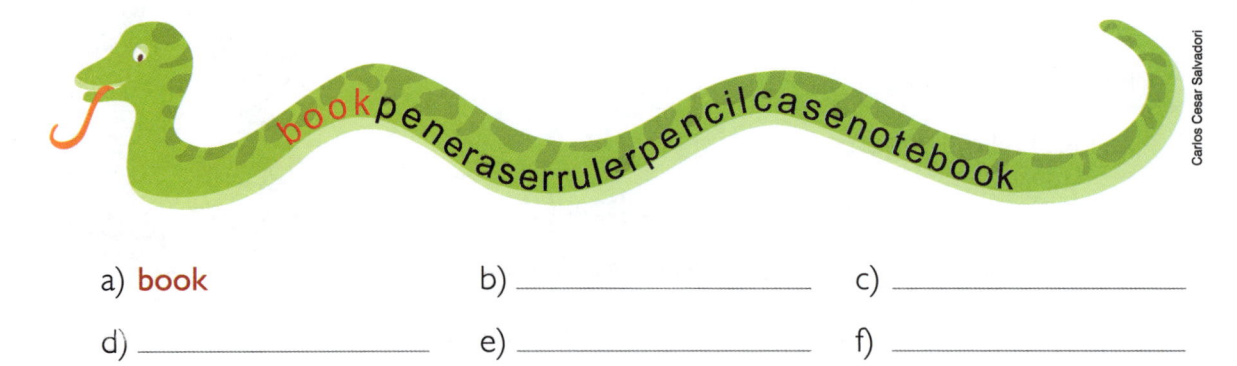

   book pen eraser ruler pencil case notebook

   a) book   b) _____   c) _____
   d) _____   e) _____   f) _____

2. Match the subjects with the corresponding book covers.

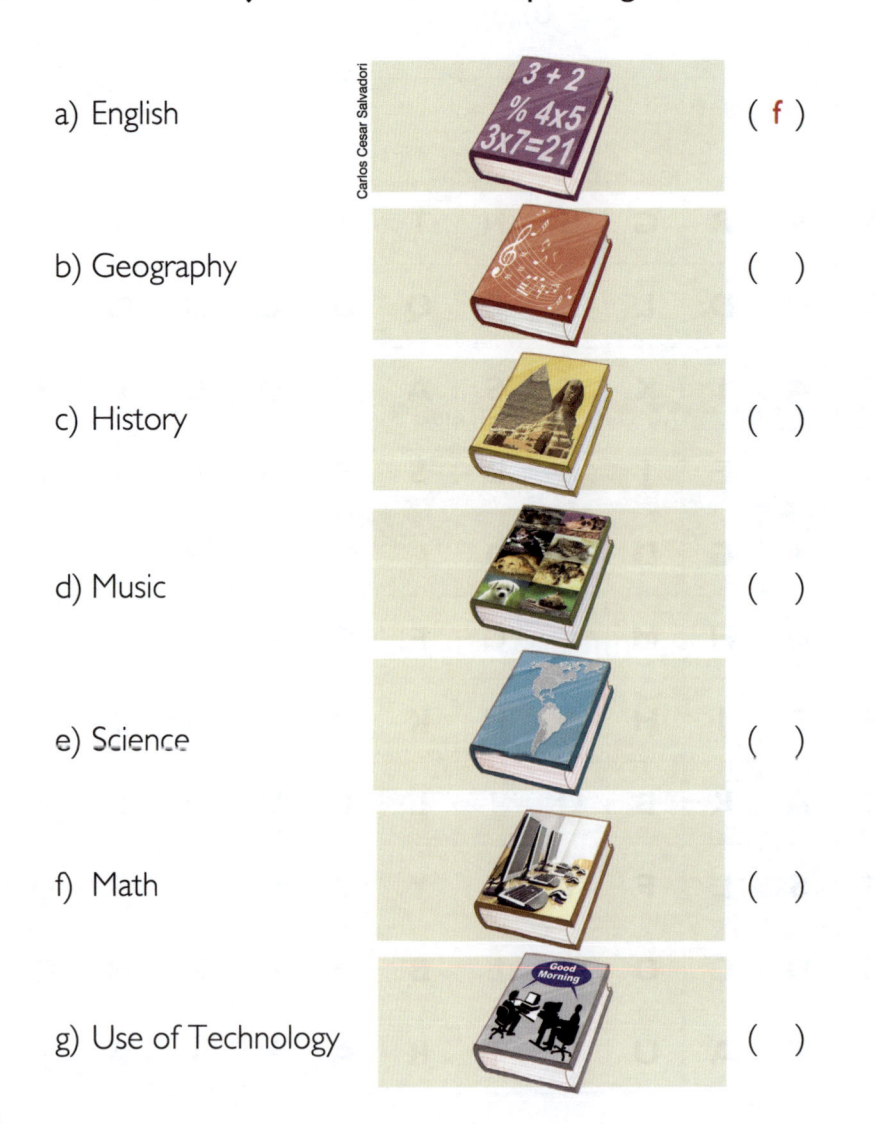

   a) English   (f)

   b) Geography   ( )

   c) History   ( )

   d) Music   ( )

   e) Science   ( )

   f) Math   ( )

   g) Use of Technology   ( )

3. Look at the table. Are the sentences True (T) or False (F)?
Monday = MON. (abbreviation)
P.E. = Physical Education

MON.	TUES.	WED.	THURS.	FRI.
English	Music	English	Art	English
Math	Math	Math	Music	Geography
Geography	Science	P.E.	Science	Library Instruction
Portuguese	P.E.	Portuguese	Spanish	Portuguese
Art	Library Instruction	Science	Spanish	Math

a) (T) English is on Monday, Wednesday and Friday.

b) (   ) Music isn't on Friday.

c) (   ) Math is on Monday, Tuesday, Wednesday and Friday.

d) (   ) Library Instruction isn't on Tuesday and Friday.

e) (   ) Spanish is on Thursday.

4. Answer the questions about the table in exercise 3. Write complete answers.

a) Is music on Tuesday and Thursday?
   Yes, it is.

b) Is art on Monday and Thursday?
   _____

c) What's on Thursday?
   _____

d) Is science on Tuesday and Friday?
   _____

e) Is P.E. on Tuesday and Wednesday?
   _____

Review — **Unit 1/2**

1. Put the sentences in the correct order to form a dialogue.

   _____ I'm Cate Campbell. And you?
   _____ No, I'm not. I'm English. And you, where are you from?
   _____ Yes, I am.
   ___1___ What's your name?
   _____ Are you American?
   _____ I'm Sarah Gibbs.
   _____ I'm from Sydney, Australia. Are you from London?

2. Look at the pictures. Read the sentences below. Copy the sentences in the corresponding balloons.

   I'm from England. – ~~Hello!~~ – No, I'm not. – I'm Gabriela.

   a) Hi! / Hello!
   b) Where are you from?
   c) Are you Brazilian?
   d) What's your name?

3. Look at the definitions below:

Sharpener: a) It's a cutting tool to sharpen pencils.
Board: b) A piece of wood hung on the wall of a classroom. You can write on it.
Desk: c) It has a writing surface. You can sit on it.

Available at: <http://dictionary.reference.com>. Access on: Jun. 8th, 2011.

4. Now guess the corresponding answers. Write the words.

   a) How do you say "apontador" in English? **Sharpener**

   b) How do you say "quadro" in English? _____

   c) How do you say "carteira escolar" in English? _____

5. Underline the sentences that are true for you.

   a) I'm from Brazil.

   b) I'm American.

   c) My favorite school subject is Use of Technology.

   d) English is on Tuesday and Thursday in my school.

   e) My teacher is from Brazil, too.

Check List – Things I can do in English

☺ I can.

😐 I don't think I can.

☹ I can't. I want to review.

- ☐ Greet people.
- ☐ Give simple instructions.
- ☐ Say my name and where I'm from.
- ☐ Say the days of the week.
- ☐ Label school subjects.
- ☐ Make a school schedule.
- ☐ Tell someone about my favorite school subject.
- ☐ Label classroom objects and personal possessions.

Unit 3

1. Look at the picture below.

2. Now answer the questions.

a) What's number 1? **It's a pencil case.**

b) What's number 2? _____

c) What's number 3? _____

d) What's number 4? _____

e) What's number 5? _____

f) What's number 6? _____

3. Look at this school's floor plan:

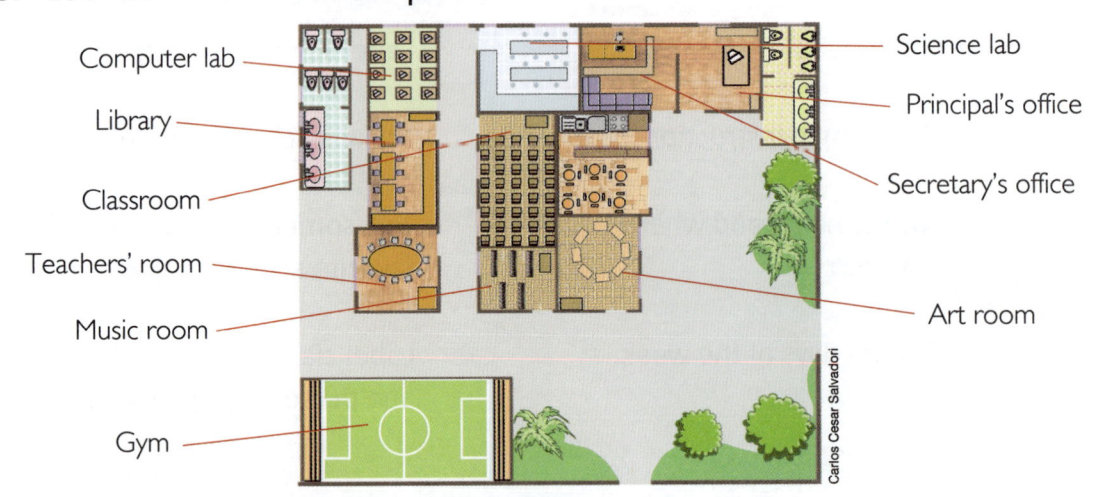

- Computer lab
- Library
- Classroom
- Teachers' room
- Music room
- Gym
- Science lab
- Principal's office
- Secretary's office
- Art room

4. Now answer the questions:

a) Where's the classroom?

    Possible answers: **It's between the music room and the science lab.**
                                    It's next to the music room.
                                    It's next to the science lab.

b) Is the music room next to the art room?

_____

c) Where's the computer lab?

_____

d) Is the classroom across from the computer lab?

_____

e) Where's the art room?

_____

f) Is the music room across from the art room?

_____

5. Read and complete the dialogue. Use the words from the box.

~~Here's your student card.~~
Thanks.
Where are you from, David?
I'm David Parker.
What's your e-mail?

ISB International School of Brazil
NAME: DAVID PARKER
CITY: WASHINGTON
COUNTRY: U.S.A.
GRADE: 6th
E-MAIL: david@isb.com.br

Miss Santos: Hi! My name is Miss Santos. What's your name?

David: _____

Miss Santos: _____

David: I'm from Washington, D.C.. I'm American. And you, where are you from Miss Santos?

Miss Santos: I'm from Brazil. _____

David: It's david@isb.com.br

Miss Santos: **Here's your student card.**

David: _____

Miss Santos: You're welcome.

Unit 4

1. Find the family members in the wordsearch below.

   a) grandfather
   b) grandmother
   c) father
   d) mother
   e) brother
   f) sister
   g) uncle
   h) aunt

W	F	X	N	J	T	Q	W	Q	W	G	Q	H	U	G	Q
Q	K	D	E	U	A	W	Z	X	B	J	K	L	N	A	D
A	L	V	F	Y	S	D	A	S	E	H	D	S	C	M	A
Z	O	B	T	J	D	F	D	D	R	F	V	D	L	G	Z
C	U	N	H	G	R	A	N	D	F	A	T	H	E	R	X
B	E	F	M	R	F	U	F	F	T	T	V	X	F	M	C
F	F	F	M	A	G	N	H	B	Y	H	F	C	H	D	V
H	G	N	C	N	H	T	L	G	U	E	H	S	K	B	B
K	J	Q	A	D	J	G	M	E	B	R	O	T	H	E	R
N	K	E	V	M	K	H	J	T	I	J	J	G	E	D	N
J	S	V	M	O	T	H	E	R	J	L	G	S	J	G	M
G	G	N	K	T	A	C	H	J	F	N	H	S	F	B	D
G	M	T	L	H	A	V	E	R	T	U	M	H	J	H	H
S	I	S	T	E	R	A	S	D	F	G	J	M	L	L	J
L	G	R	S	R	A	S	D	F	G	H	J	T	Y	O	D
F	H	J	R	Q	W	E	R	T	Y	U	I	O	P	R	O

2. Complete the chart:

Full Form	Short Form
I am Daisy.	
He is George.	
	She's Susan.
It is Fluffy.	

3. Write sentences.

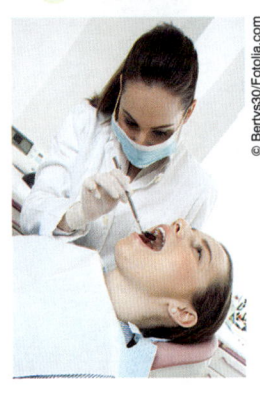

a) She's a dentist.

b) _____

c) _____

d) _____

4. Write questions and answers.

a) Who's she? She's Sarah.

b) _____ He's David.

c) Where's he from? _____

d) What's her name? _____

e) _____ His name is Ricardo.

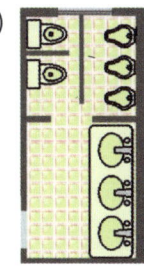

f) _____ It's next to the girls' room.

107

Review Unit 3/4

1. Read and complete.

   a) What's four plus ten? **(4 + 10 = 14)**
      It's fourteen.

   b) What's seven plus eleven? _____

   c) What's thirteen plus twelve? _____

   d) What's thirty minus eleven? _____

   e) What's twenty-seven minus fourteen? _____

2. Write the rooms at a school in alphabetical order.

   > teacher's room – music room – principal's office – classroom – cafeteria – girls' room – art room – library – gym – computer lab – science lab – boys' room – secretary's office

   art room
   _____
   _____
   _____
   _____
   _____

3. Can you find six professions in the word search?

W	F	E	N	G	I	N	E	E	R	G	A	G	D	G	A
A	K	D	E	U	A	W	Z	X	B	J	K	L	I	A	R
D	L	V	F	Y	S	D	A	S	E	H	D	S	L	M	C
S	O	B	T	J	D	S	T	U	D	E	N	T	Ç	G	H
O	U	N	H	D	S	W	F	S	K	L	R	T	L	D	I
C	E	F	M	V	F	U	F	F	T	T	V	X	F	M	T
C	S	B	U	S	I	N	E	S	S	W	O	M	A	N	E
E	G	N	C	S	H	T	L	G	U	D	H	S	K	B	C
R	J	Q	A	D	J	G	M	E	B	H	O	F	H	E	T
P	K	E	V	M	K	H	J	T	I	A	J	D	E	D	F
L	S	V	M	Y	T	H	R	J	J	F	G	O	J	G	G
A	G	N	K	B	A	C	H	J	F	N	H	C	F	B	F
Y	M	T	L	T	A	V	E	R	T	U	M	T	J	H	C
E	D	F	H	Y		A	S	D	F	G	J	O	L	L	J
R	G	R	S	D	A	S	D	F	G	H	J	R	Y	O	D

4. Now copy the professions here.

   a) businesswoman

   b) engineer

   c) student

   d) architect

   e) soccer player

   f) doctor

Check List – Things I can do in English

☺ I can.

😐 I don't think I can.

☹ I can't. I want to review.

☐ Count from 1 to 30.

☐ Label rooms at school.

☐ Say the English alphabet.

☐ Describe people and family relationships.

☐ Spell words and names.

☐ Describe people and their professions.

Unit 5

1. Match the corresponding numbers.

   forty-two
   fifty-seven
   sixty-one
   seventy-four
   eighty-nine
   ninety-five
   a hundred and twenty-three

   74   57   95   61   123   89   42

2. Now color the numbers with the corresponding colors.

   a) Forty-two is black.
   b) Fifty-seven is pink.
   c) Sixty-one is yellow.
   d) Seventy-four is blue.
   e) Eight-nine is red.
   f) Ninety-five is orange.
   g) A hundred and twenty-three is green.

3. Answer the questions. Write the numbers in full.

   a) How much is an apple?
   It's fifty cents.

   US$ 0.50

   b) How much is a sandwich?
   _____

   R$ 5,00

   c) How much is a soda?
   _____

   US$ 1.20

   d) How much is a bottle of water?
   _____

   R$ 1,75

4. Circle the correct negative form.

   a) David **is not** / are not from the USA.

   b) Gabriela and Ricardo is not / are not from Japan.

   c) Mrs. Costa is not / are not a student. She's a teacher.

   d) Sarah, Laura and Cate is not / are not dentists. They're students.

   e) Lyndon is not / are not English. He's South African.

5. Put the words in the correct order to make questions. Then answer the questions. Use short forms.

   a) Kazuki / Japan / is / from
   Is Kazuki from Japan?
   Yes, he is.

   b) Cate / Australian / is
   _____

   c) Are / Ricardo / Gabriela/ Brazil / from / and
   _____

   d) Kazuki / Lyndon / David / students / are / and
   _____

6. Answer the questions.

   a) Are you a student?
   _____

   b) Is your English teacher from Brazil?
   _____

   c) Are your parents teachers?
   _____

   d) Is breakfast your favorite meal?
   _____

   e) Is soda your favorite drink?
   _____

Unit 6

1. Correct the mistakes in each sentence:

   a) English class is in Monday. **on**

   b) My birthday is at August 22ⁿᵈ. _____

   c) New Year's Eve is on December. _____

   d) My school is at Madison Avenue. _____

   e) My house is on 192 Oak Street. _____

2. Complete the table with the months of the year.

BRAZIL (SEASONS)	MONTHS	CANADA
☀ (sun)	January February _____	❄ (snowflake)
🍂 (leaf)	_____ May _____	🌺 (flower)
❄ (snowflake)	July August	☀ (sun)
🌺 (flower)	September October _____	🍂 (leaf)

3. Now complete the sentences about months and seasons in Brazil and Canada.

   a) In Canada summer is from **June** to **September**.

   b) In Brazil winter is from _____ to _____.

   c) In Canada fall is from _____ to _____.

   d) In Brazil summer is from _____ to _____.

   e) In Brazil spring is from _____ to _____.

   f) In Canada winter is from _____ to _____.

4. Look at the table in exercise 2 again. Are the sentences true (T) or false (F)?

a) It's hot in Brazil in July. (**F**)
b) It's cold in Canada in February. ( )
c) It's freezing in Canada in December. ( )
d) It's warm in Brazil in September. ( )
e) It's freezing in Brazil in January. ( )

5. Write and color the clothes.

jeans

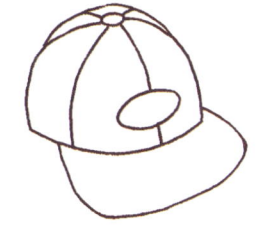

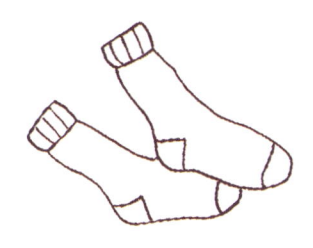

a) Green jeans
c) A purple T-Shirt
e) An orange coat
g) Blue shoes
i) White socks

b) A pink and yellow dress
d) Gray shorts
f) Black and red sneakers
h) A brown cap

Review Unit 5/6

1. Match the questions and the answers.

a) Where are you from?
b) Are you Japanese?
c) Is geography your favorite subject?
d) Where is the library?
e) Who's she?
f) Is your father an architect?
g) Are Gabriela and Miss Santos from Argentina?

( ) No, I'm not. I'm Australian.
( ) She's my aunt.
( ) It's next to the classroom, across from the boys' room.
(a) I'm from Italy.
( ) No, he isn't. He's a history teacher.
( ) No, it isn't. It's Math.
( ) No, they aren't. They are from Brazil.

2. Unscramble the letters. Write the words.

a) N-N-A-A-A-S-B = bananas

b) S-T-R-R-C-A-O = _____

c) P-S-E-L-P-A = _____

d) T-S-A-E-O-O-M-T = _____

e) E-E-E-R-R-S-B-U-I-L-B = _____

f) M-N-O-E-S-L = _____

g) G-O-S-A-E-R-N = _____

114

3. Match the symbols to the sentences describing weather and temperature.

WEATHER

a) It's windy.
b) It's cloudy.
c) It's snowy.
d) It's sunny.
e) It's rainy.

TEMPERATURE

a) 0 °C — It's hot.
b) 35 °C — It's warm.
c) 7 °C — It's freezing.
d) 23 °C — It's cold.

4. What's your favorite kind of weather?

_____

5. What's your favorite season?

_____

Check List – Things I can do in English

☺ I can.

☺ I don't think I can.

☹ I can't. I want to review.

☐ Count from 1 to 100.
☐ Describe and talk about the weather.
☐ Label and talk about some food and drink for breakfast, lunch and dinner.
☐ Read weather symbols.
☐ Describe items of clothing.
☐ Make a menu in English.
☐ Talk about possessions.

115

Unit 7

1. Look at the city map.

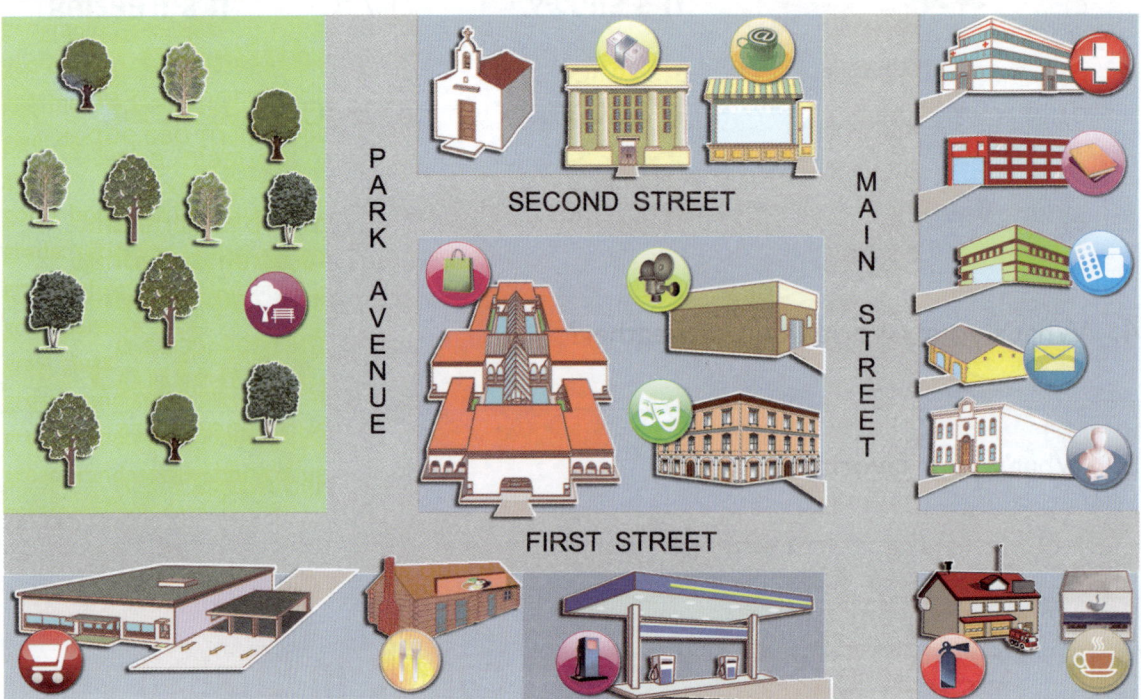

Shopping Mall | Supermarket | Fire Station | Coffee Shop | Museum | Hospital | Internet Café | Post Office
Restaurant | Gas Station | Drugstore | Movie Theater | Bookstore | Park | Bank | Theater

PARK AVENUE — SECOND STREET — FIRST STREET — MAIN STREET

2. Now answer the questions about the map.

a) Is there a drugstore between the bookstore and the museum?

No, there isn't. There's a drugstore between the bookstore and the post office.

b) Is there a bank behind the restaurant?

___

c) Is there a restaurant across from the church?

___

d) Is there a fire station next to the park?

___

e) Is there an internet café on the corner of Main Street and First Street?

_____

_____

3. Look at the map again. Are the sentences True (T) or False (F)?

a) (T) The museum is on Main Street.
b) (   ) The post office is across from the movie theater.
c) (   ) The church is on the corner of Second Street and First Street.
d) (   ) The theater is behind the coffee shop.
e) (   ) The gas station is on the corner of First Street and Main Street.

4. What time is it?

a) 09:00   It's nine o'clock.

b) 10:30   _____

c) 02:00   _____

d) 05:00   _____

e) 07:30   _____

5. Circle the word that doesn't belong.

a) a refrigerator – a stove – a microwave – (a dining room)

b) a table – a shower – a chair – a dining room

c) a shower – a sink – a toilet – a living room

d) a living room – a sofa – a TV set – a stove

e) a bedroom – a bed – a toilet – a wardrobe – a desk

Unit 8

1. Match the questions and the answers.

a) What's your favorite drink? ( ) It's hot and sunny.

b) Where are you from? ( ) No, I'm not. I'm an engineer.

c) How's the weather? ( ) No, I can't.

d) Can you ride a horse? (a) It's coffee and milk.

e) Are you a doctor? ( ) It's 329-7418.

f) What's your telephone number? ( ) I'm from Rome, Italy.

2. Circle the best responses.

1. How much is it?
   a) It's rainy.
   b) It's five reais and twenty cents. *(circled)*
   c) It's in the afternoon.

2. What time is it?
   a) It's at 159 Pine Street.
   b) It's across from the gym.
   c) It's four-thirty.

3. Where's the internet café?
   a) It's Ricardo's.
   b) It's behind the bookstore.
   c) It's at night.

4. Can a bird sing?
   a) Yes, it is.
   b) Yes, I can.
   c) Yes, it can.

3. Complete with the correct prepositions: **in**, **on**, or **at**.

   a) My classes are **in** the morning.
   b) The basketball game is _____ five o'clock _____ Sunday afternoon.
   c) The concert is _____ night.
   d) The picnic is _____ Saturday.
   e) The English test is _____ March 2nd.
   f) Summer in Brazil is _____ December, January and February.

4. Talk to your classmates.

   A: Who can ride a horse?
   B: **Julia** can ride a horse.

Find someone who can	Name(s)
Sing and dance hip hop	
Swim	
Draw and paint	
Play the guitar	
Skateboard	
Play volleyball	

5. Match

   a) A dog   can swim.
   b) A bird   can jump.
   c) A cat   can walk on four legs.
   d) A parrot   can sing.
   e) Fish   can talk.
   f) A rabbit   can run very fast.

Review Unit 7/8

1. Look at these events.

Orchestra Concert – Millenaris Theater
Friday evening – 6:30 p.m.

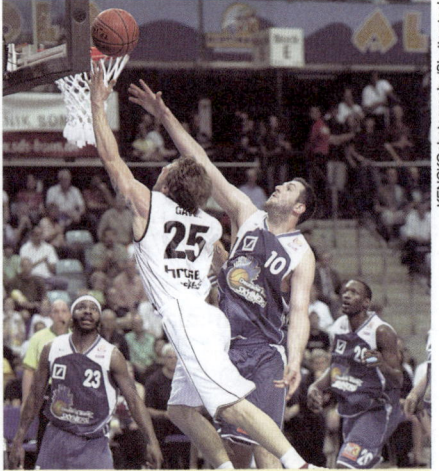

Basketball Game – City Stadium
Wednesday – 10:00 a.m.

Picnic – Green Park –
Sunday afternoon – 3:00 p.m.

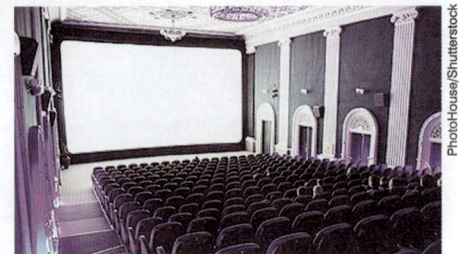

Movie Session – Cineplex
Saturday night – 10:00 p.m.

2. What time are the events? Complete the sentences.

a) The band concert is **on** Friday.

b) The band concert is _____ 6:30 p.m.

c) The picnic _____ the afternoon. It isn't _____ the morning.

d) The movie session is _____ Saturday night.

e) The movie session is not _____ the afternoon. It's _____ night.

3. Where are these events? Write sentences:

a) The orchestra concert is at the Millenaris Theater.

b) _____

c) _____

d) _____

4. Answer the questions.

a) Can you speak Spanish? _____

b) Can your mother make a cake? _____

c) Can your father play volleyball? _____

d) Can your English teacher play the piano? _____

e) Can you play table tennis? _____

5. Complete the information about yourself.

My full name is _____

My nationality is _____

My city is _____

My country is _____

My favorite school subject is _____

My favorite food is _____

My favorite drink is _____

I can speak _____

I can _____

Check List – Things I can do in English

🙂 I can.

😐 I don't think I can.

🙁 I can't. I want to review.

☐ Talk about my neighborhood.

☐ Talk about locations in a city.

☐ Give an address.

☐ Give directions.

☐ Describe things and rooms in a house.

☐ Tell the time.

How do you say… in English?

1. How do you say "estar com saudades" in English?

   I miss my grandparents.

2. How do you say "mãe coruja" in English?

   I'm proud of Laura. I'm a doting mother.

3. How do you say "decorar" in English?

   What about the geography test?

   I know the capitals by heart.

   The capital of Brazil is Brasília.

4. How do you say "comes e bebes" in English?

Come and join us at ISB!
Country Party on June 24th
Attire: Country clothing
Let's have some snacks and drinks together.
Don't miss!

5. How do you say "estar com saudades de casa" in English?

I feel homesick.

6. How do you say "mais vale um pássaro na mão do que dois voando" in English?

"A bird in the hand is worth two in the bush."

Project 1

ENGLAND:
It is a country that is part of the United Kingdom (UK). It's in Europe.

English people speak English in England.

London is the capital of England.

London

FOOD

FISH AND CHIPS
It's the most popular food in UK and areas colonized by British people.

DRINK

A CUP OF TEA
English people like to have tea and biscuits at teatime.

WESTMINSTER ABBEY
It's the traditional place of coronation and burial site for British monarchs in London.

BIG BEN
It's the world's most famous clock tower. It's a very important symbol of both London and England.

English people love football.

124

Project 2

My grandparents are Portuguese.

Grandparents
- **Grandfather:** Paulo Melo
- **Grandmother:** Tania Melo

Grandparents
- **Grandfather:** Rafael Silva
- **Grandmother:** Sara Aguiar Silva

Parents
- **Uncle:** Julio Melo
- **Mother:** Patrícia Melo Silva
- **Father:** Manoel Silva
- **Aunt:** Lúcia Silva

Gabriela is Pedro's sister.

- Gabriela Silva
- **Brother:** Pedro Silva

This is Gabriela's family tree.

PORTUGUESE FAMILY NAMES
- **AGUIAR**
  It comes from Latin *Aguilare* (related to an eagle).
- **SILVA**
  It comes from Latin. It means "forest" or "jungle".

available at. <www.benzlsobrenomes.com/nomes/princ.htm>. Access on: Jun. 22th, 2011.

And you?
Where are your great-grandparents / grandparents from?

Look at some important contributions from Portuguese immigrants to Brazil.

NATIVE LANGUAGE: People speak Portuguese in Brazil.

FOOD: There are many bakers in Brazil that come from Portugal.

ARCHITECTURE: Colonial architectural styles, in Paraty (RJ).

FESTIVALS: There are festivals in June in Brazil. They came from Portugal.

Project 3

HOW TO MAKE A RESTAURANT FLYER

1. Think about interesting places to eat in the city where you live.

2. Select one of them. Think about how interesting it is and the kind of food they serve.

3. Write down the name of the restaurant, the address, telephone numbers and website.

4. Pretend you have just been hired to create a flyer for this restaurant. Here's a model for you.

Restaurant Mister Grill

Come and visit us!

Cuisine: Brazilian ("Churrasco", park ribs, chicken thighs, Brazilian sausage, "feijoada" (black bean stew)

Business Hours
Dress code: elegant
Payment option: Credit card or cash

1240 Sunset Boulevard, Los Angeles, CA 90010 - Phone: (213) 347-1850 - Fax: (213) 321-7925
E-mail: www.mistergrill.com

Now it's your turn

1. Provide a sheet of paper in case you want to do it in a written way. Use the sample above as a model for you.

2. If you intend to do it on your computer think about pictures, different sizes and kinds of letters. Use your creativity.

3. Show your flyer to the class.

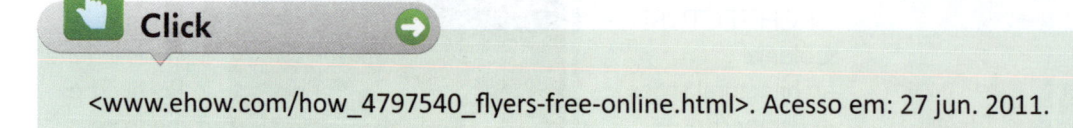

Click

<www.ehow.com/how_4797540_flyers-free-online.html>. Acesso em: 27 jun. 2011.
A site where you can create flyers for free online. Then you can print your flyer.

Project 4

SPORTS AROUND THE WORLD: SOCCER

A SOCCER PLAYER

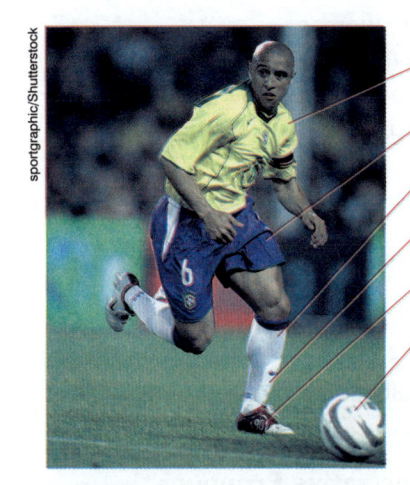

- TEAM SHIRT
- SHORTS
- SOCK
- SHIN GUARD
- SOCCER SHOES
- SOCCER BALL

GOALKEEPER'S GLOVES

Roberto Carlos, a famous Brazilian soccer player.
Who is your favorite soccer play?

Don't miss!

<http://pt.fifa.com/>. Access on: October 26th, 2011. FIFA'S website in Portuguese.

Places: It's the most popular sport in Brazil.
Soccer rules: They were codified in England by the Football Association in 1863.
Players: There are eleven players in each team.
Rules: The team that scores more goals at the end of the game is the winner.
Where people play it: On a soccer field.

Soccer, football or rugby?
- American football is from the United States of America.
- Soccer originated in England. Soccer is played in Brazil.
- Rugby: type of football where you can hold the ball in your hands and kick the ball.

HOW TO MAKE YOUR POSTER

1. Select a popular sport around the world.
2. Say where it is played.
3. Show the uniform.
4. How is it played?
5. Who are the most famous players of this sport?

Grammar Points

Articles

A. The indefinite article – A/ AN
- Only with singular countable nouns
- Before a consonant sound: A a pen
- Before a vowel sound or silent 'H': AN
  an apple   an honest man

B. The definite article – THE
- It can be used for masculine and feminine:
  the man   the woman
- It can be used with singular and plural nouns:
  the book   the students
- It can be used for countable and uncountable nouns:
  the boys   the coffee

Nouns

Masculine: boy   feminine: girl
Neuter: cat
Singular: boy, girl, cat
Plural: boys, girls, cats

Adjectives

- Use adjectives to describe nouns or pronouns.
  The **houses** are beautiful. They are **new**.
- Adjectives usually come before nouns. This is a **small** kitchen.

Pronouns

Personal	Possessive + Nouns
I	My
You	Your
He	His
She	Her
It	Its
We	Our
You	Your
They	Their

Demonstrative Pronouns

THIS, THESE (near)	THAT, THOSE (far)

This is my notebook.
There are my dogs.
That is our teacher.
Those are your parents.

Numbers in English

0 zero	1 one	2 two	3 three	4 four	5 five	6 six	7 seven	8 eight	9 nine
ten	eleven	twelve	thirteen	fourteen	fifteen	sixteen	seventeen	eighteen	nineteen
twenty	twenty-one	twenty-two	twenty-three	twenty-four	twenty-five	twenty-six	twenty-seven	twenty-eight	twenty-nine
thirty	thirty-two								
forty			forty-three						
fifty				fifty-four					
sixty					sixty-five				
seventy						seventy-six			
eighty							eighty-seven		
ninety								ninety-eight	
one / a hundred									

Ordinal Numbers

1st	first	11th	eleventh	21st	twenty-first
2nd	second	12th	twelfth	22nd	twenty-second
3rd	third	13th	thirteenth	23rd	twenty-third
4th	fourth	14th	fourteenth	24th	twenty-fourth
5th	fifth	15th	fifteenth	25th	twenty-fifth
6th	sixth	16th	sixteenth	26th	twenty-sixth
7th	seventh	17th	seventeenth	27th	twenty-seventh
8th	eighth	18th	eighteenth	28th	twenty-eighth
9th	ninth	19th	nineteenth	29th	twenty-ninth
10th	tenth	20th	twentieth	30th	thirtieth

There + to be

Affirmative singular: There is a backpack in the classroom. (existence of something)
Affirmative plural: There are ten students in the library. (presence of someone)
Negative singular: There isn't a cat in the bedroom.
Negative plural: There aren't any girls in the girls' room.
Interrogative plural: Are there any oranges in the refrigerator?

Question words with the verb To Be

What is your name? My name is Sarah.
What is your telephone number? It's 9741-3620.
Where is she from? She's from Brazil.
What is your favorite subject? It's history.
What is the day today? It's Monday.
What is in your backpack? Pens, pencil and ruler.
What is this? It's an eraser.
What are these? They're erasers.
What subject is this? It's Math.
Where is the lab? It's next to the gym.
Who is from South Africa? Lyndon is.
Who is he? He's my father.
Who are they? They're my grandparents.
What time is the concert? It's at 4:00 p.m.
What color is the coat? It's black and gray.
How much is this yogurt? It's US $3.50.
How is the weather? It's sunny and hot.

Prepositions

PLACE: indicate where someone or something is:
The students are <u>in</u> the classroom.
Gabriela is <u>at</u> home.
The school is <u>on</u> Pine Street.

DIRECTION: indicate where someone or something is:
The hospital is <u>behind</u> the drugstore.
The cafeteria is <u>next to</u> the lab.
The bedroom is <u>across from</u> the bathroom.
The bookstore is <u>between</u> the church and the bank.
The theater is <u>on the corner of</u> Main Street and First Street.

TIME:
The soccer game is <u>on</u> Sunday at 5:00 p.m.
Summer in Brazil is <u>in</u> January.

To be

Interrogative
Am I…?
Are you…?
Is he…?
Is she…?
Is it…?
Are we…?
Are you…?
Are they…?

Affirmative
I am = I'm
You are = You're
He is = He's
She is = She's
It is = It's
We are = We're
You are = You're
They are = They're

Negative
I am not = I'm not
You're not = you aren't
He's not = he isn't
She's not = she isn't
It's not = it isn't
We're not = we aren't
You're not = you aren't
They're not = they aren't

Modal verb Can (ability)

- Use can to talk about ability in the present: I can ride a bike.

Interrogative
- Can she play the piano?

Affirmative
- I can speak French.

Negative
- They can't dance.

129

Glossary

A

able-bodied: capaz
about: cerca de
above: acima
abroad: no exterior
access: acesso
accessible: acessível
according to: segundo
achieve: atingir
across from: em frente de
activity: atividade
add: somar
address: endereço
advertise: fazer propaganda
afford: dar se ao luxo de
afternoon: tarde
again: novamente
against: contra
age: idade
agree: concordar
aim: objetivo
airport: aeroporto
alphabetical: alfabético(a)
also: também
American: americano(a)
among: entre (mais de dois)
answer: resposta / responder
any: alguns, algumas, nenhum(a)
anything: algo
apartment: apartamento
apologize: desculpar-se
appealing: atraente
appear: aparecer
appetizer: aperitivo
apple: maçã
appliances: louças de cozinha e banheiro
architect: arquiteto(a)
Argentinean: argentino(a)
around: ao redor
art: arte
article: artigo
ask: perguntar
association: associação
at: em, a
attend: frequentar
attention: atenção
attribute: atributo
aunt: tia
Australian: australiano(a)

B

back: parte de trás
backpack: mochila
backwards: para trás
bad: ruim
balloon: balão
bank: banco
barrier: barreira
bathroom: banheiro
bean: feijão
beautiful: lindo(a)
bed: cama
bedroom: quarto
before: antes
begin: começar
behind: atrás de
believe: acreditar
belong: pertencer
below: abaixo
belt: cinto
between: entre (2 coisas/pessoas)
bicycle: bicicleta
big: grande
bird: pássaro
birthday party: festa de aniversário
black: preto(a)
blood pressure: pressão arterial
blouse: camisa feminina
blue: azul
blueberries: mirtilo
board: quadro
boat: barco
body: corpo
book: livro
bookstore: livraria
bottle: garrafa
box: caixa de texto
boy: menino
Brazilian: brasileiro(a)
bread: pão
break time: recreio
breakfast: café da manhã
British: britânico(a)
broccoli: brócolis
brother: irmão
brown: marrom
brush: escova
businesswoman: mulher de negócios
busy: ocupado(a)
but: mas

C

cafeteria: cantina
cake: bolo
calculator: calculadora
calendar: calendário
calories: calorias
can: poder
cap: boné
capital letter: letra maiúscula
card: cartão, carteira
carrot: cenoura
cat: gato
catch: pegar
celebrity: celebridade
cell phone: celular
chair: cadeira
change: trocar
charade: charada
chart: tabela
chat: bater papo
cheap: barato(a)
check: examinar
cheese: queijo
chicken: carne de frango
children: crianças
Chinese: chinês(a)
cholesterol: colesterol
choose: escolher
church: igreja
circle: circular
city: cidade
class: classe
classmate: colega
classroom: sala de aula

clean: limpar
clenched fist: punho cerrado
click: clicar
close: fechar
closely: de perto
clothing: vestuário
cloudy: nublado
coat: casaco
code: código
coffee: café
coffee shop: café
cold: frio(a)
color: cor
comfortable: confortável
common: comum
communicate: comunicar
communication: comunicação
compare: comparar
complete: completar
computer: computador
conceive: conceber
concert: concerto
condition: condição
conflict: conflito
connect: conectar
contact: contato
contain: conter
control: controlar
conversation: conversa
cookie: bolacha doce
copy: copiar
corner: esquina
correct: correto(a)
corresponding: correspondente
correspondingly: de forma correspondente
country: país
cousin: primo(a)
cover: capa, cobrir
create: criar
cross out: riscar
culture: cultura
cut: cortar

D

daily: diariamente
dangerous: perigoso(a)
date: data
day: dia
dear: querido(a)
definition: definição
degree: grau
deliver: entregar
dentist: dentista
describe: descrever
description: descrição
design: desenhar
desk: carteira escolar com braço, escrivaninha
dessert: sobremesa
determine: determinar
dialogue: diálogo
difference: diferença
different: diferente
digital: digital
dining room: sala de jantar
dinner: almoço
disability: incapacidade
discount: desconto
discuss: discutir
disease: doença
divide: dividir
doctor: médico(a)
dog: cachorro
door: porta
downtown: centro da cidade
draw: desenhar
dress: vestido
drink: bebida
drugstore: farmácia que vende remédios e comida
dry: seco(a)
duke: duque

E

easily: facilmente
eat: comer
emotion: emoção
engineer: engenheiro(a)
English: inglês(a), língua inglesa
enroll: matricular-se
enter: entrar
eraser: borracha
even: mesmo
evening: final de tarde
examine: examinar
exchange: trocar
excuse: desculpe
exercise: exercício
exercise: exercitar
exhibition: exposição
expensive: caro(a)

F

fact: fato
fall: outono
false: falso(a)
family: família
family tree: árvore genealógica
famous: famoso(a)
fast: rápido(a)
fast food: comida rápida
fat: gordura
father: pai
favorite: favorito(a)
feet: pés
find: encontrar
finish: término
fire station: corpo de bombeiros
first: primeiro(a)
fish: peixe
fit: encaixar
flag: bandeira
floor plan: planta baixa
fly: voar
foggy: nevoento
food: comida
foreign: estrangeiro(a)
forget: esquecer
forgive: perdoar
forgiveness: perdão
forwards: para frente
freezing: gelado(a)
french fries: batata frita
French: francês(a), língua francesa
Friday: sexta-feira
fried: frito(a)
friend: amigo(a)
from: (procedência) de
frozen: congelado(a)

fruit: fruta
fun: diversão
furniture: mobília

G

game: jogo
gap: lacuna
garage: garagem
garlic: alho
gas station: posto de gasolina
generally: geralmente
geography: geografia
get: conseguir, obter
girl: menina
give: dar
go: ir
good: bom, boa
grade: série, ano
grandfather: avô
grandparents: avós
gray: cinza
great-grandfather: bisavô
great-grandmother: bisavó
great-grandparents: bisavós
greatness: grandeza
green: verde
grilled: grelhado(a)
guess: adivinhar
guide: guia
guitar: violão
gym: ginásio

H

ham: presunto
hand: mão
hangman: forca
hard: difícil
have: ter
he: ele
health: saúde
healthy: saudável
hear: ouvir
hearing impaired person: surdo(a)
heart: coração
hello: oi, oláhelp: ajudar
her: dela
here: aqui

hi: oi, olá
high: alto(a)
hint: dica
his: dele
history: história
home: casa, lar
horse: cavalo
hot: calor
hot dog: cachorro quente
house: casa
how: como
how many: quantos(as)
how much: quanto custa(preço)
hungry: com fome
hurt: machucar

I

I: eu
ice cream: sorvete
ID: carteira de identidade
idea: ideia
identify: identificar
igloo: iglu
illustration: ilustração
imagine: imaginar
impaired person: pessoa com necessidade especial
important: importante
include: incluir
inevitable: inevitável
instruction: instrução
insult: insultar
internet café: cybercafé
involve: envolver
Irish: irlandês(a)
issue: assunto
its: dele, dela

J

jacket: jaqueta, paletó
Japanese: japonês(a)
join: juntar-se
juice: sucojump: pular
junk food: lanche sem valor nutritivo

K

keep: guardar
keyword: palavra-chave
kill: matar
kind: tipo
kitchen: cozinha
know: saber, conhecer

L

lab: laboratório
label: identificar, nomear
lamp: lâmpada, lustre
language: língua
last: último(a)
learn: aprender
leave: deixar
leg: perna
lemonade: limonada
lesson: lição
let's: vamos
letter: letra
level: nível
library: biblioteca
life: vida
like: gostar
limit: limite
list: list
listen: escutar
little: pequeno(a)
living room: sala de estar
location: lugar
long: comprido(a)
look: olhar
love: amar
lower case: letra minúscula
lunch: almoço

M

main courses: pratos principais
make: fazer
man: homem
map: mapa
married: casado(a)
mashed potatoes: purê de batatas
match: relacionar
math: matemática

may, might: poder
mean: significar
meaning: significado
measure: medir
meet: encontrar
member: membro
men: homens
mess: bagunça
mice: camundongos
microwave: microondas
milk: leite
mind: mente
minus: menos
minute: minuto
miss: perder
mobile home: casa trailer
Monday: segunda-feira
monkey: macaco
month: mês
more: mais
morning: manhã
mother: mãe
motorbike: motocicleta
movie theater: cinema
multiply: multiplicar
museum: museu
music: música
must: imprescindível
my: meu(s), minha(s)

N

name: nome
nationality: nacionalidade
need: precisar
new: novo(a)
next to: ao lado de
nice: bonito(a)
night: noite
non-profit: sem fins lucrativos
note: nota
notebook: caderno
noun: substantivo
now: agora
number: número
nursing home: asilo

O

obesity: obesidade
object: objeto
observe: observar
occasion: ocasião
office: escritório, consultório
often: geralmente
on: em, sobre
onion: cebola
open: abrir
opinion: opinião
orange: laranja
order: ordem
other: outro(s), outra(s)
our: nosso(a), nossos(as)
overcome: superar

P

page: página
paint: pintar
pair: dupla
parents: pais
park: parque
parrot: papagaio
part: parte
passport: passaporte
password: senha
pasta: massa
pay: pagar
peace: paz
pen: caneta
pencil case: penal, estojo
pencil: lápis
people: pessoas
permission: permissão
pet: animal de estimação
phone: telefone
picture: figura
pie: torta
piece: pedaço
pink: rosa
place: lugar
play: brincar, tocar um instrumento
play: peça de teatro
player: jogador(a)
please: por favor
plus: mais
point: apontar
polite: apropriado(a)
Portuguese: língua portuguesa
Portuguese: português(a)
possible: possível
post office: correio
poster: cartaz
practice: praticar
prefer: preferir
prepare: preparar
preposition: preposição
previous: anterior
price: preço
prince: príncipe
princess: princesa
principal: diretor(a)
print: imprimir
problem: problema
profession: profissão
promote: promover
promotion: promoção
pronunciation: pronúncia
provide: providenciar
pudding: pudim
purple: roxo
put: colocar

Q

queen: rainha
question: pergunta
quickly: rapidamente
quotation: citação

R

rabbit: coelho
rainy: chuvoso(a)
rarely: raramente
rat: rato
read: ler
ready: pronto
really: realmentered: vermelho
refer: referir-se
refrigerator: geladeira
region: região

register: registar
relate: relacionar
relation: relação
relationship: relação
remember: lembrar-se
repeat: repetir
replace: substituir
report card: boletim
require: precisar
respect: respeitar
response: resposta
result: resultado
review: revisar
rice: arroz
riddle: charada
ride: andar de
right: certo(a)
ring: anel
roast: assado(a)
role: papel (a imitar)
room: quarto, sala
round: redondo(a)
royal: real
ruler: régua
run: correr

S

safe: seguro(a)
salad: salada
sale: liquidação
same: mesmo(a)
Saturday: sábado
say: dizer
scale: escala
scene: cena
schedule: horário
school: escola
science: ciências
Scotsman: escocês(a)
scrap: rascunho scrapbook: álbum de fotografia com legenda
season: estação do ano
secret: secreto(a)
secretary: secretária(o)

section: seção
see: ver
send: enviar
sentence: frase
serve: servir
session: sessão
shake: sacudir
share: compartilhar
sharpener: apontador
she: ela
shopping mall: centro comercial
shorts: shorts
should: deveria
show: mostrar
shower: chuveiro
sign: assinar
similar: similar
site: site (internet)
similarity: similaridade
sing: cantar
single: solteiro(a)
sink: pia
sister: irmã
skateboard: andar de skate
small: pequeno(a)
snack: lanches
sneakers: tênis
snowy: nevoso(a)
so: então
soccer: futebol jogado no Brasil
socks: meias
soda: refrigerante
sodium: sódio
solve: resolver
some: uns, umas, alguns, algumas
sometimes: às vezes
sorry: sinto muito
sound: som
soup: sopa
South African: sul-africano(a)
Spanish: língua espanhola
Spanish: espanhol(a)
speak: falar
speaker: falante
specialized: especializado

spell: soletrar
spend: gastar
spring: primavera
start: início, iniciar
starve: passar fome
station: estação
steak: bife, filé
step aside: deixar passar
store: loja
stormy: tempestuoso(a)
story: história
stove: fogão
street: rua
strong: forte
student: aluno(a)
study: estudar
subject: disciplina
subtitle: legenda
subtract: subtrair
summer: verão
Sunday: domingo
sunny: ensolarado(a)
supermarket: supermercado
surface: superfície
sweater: suéter
sweatpants: calça de moletom
sweatshirt: blusa de moletom
swim: nadar
symbol: símbolo

T

T-shirt: camiseta
table: mesa, tabela
tablet: dispositivo eletrônico pessoal em formato de prancheta
table tennis: ping pong
talk: conversar
tea: chá
teach: ensinar
teacher: professor(a)
technology: tecnologia
teen: adolescente
telephone: telefone
tell: contar
tennis: tênis (esporte)

test: teste, prova
text: texto
text message: mensagem de texto
thank you: obrigado(a)
thanks: obrigado(a)
that: aquele, aquela
the: a, o, as, os
theater: teatro
their: deles, delas
then: então
there: lá
there are: existem
there is: existe, há
these: esses, essas, estes, estas
they: eles, elas
thing: coisa
think: achar, pensar
thirsty: com sede
this: esse, essa, este, esta
those: aqueles, aquelas
Thursday: quinta-feira
time: hora, momento
times: vezes
tissues: lenços de papel
today: hoje
toilet: patente, privada
tomato: tomate
tool: instrumento
top: cobertura
touchscreen: tela de toque
track: faixa do CD
translation: tradução
travel: viajar
true: verdadeiro(a)
try: tentar
Tuesday: terça-feira
turn on: ligar
turn: vez
TV set: aparelho de TV
type: tipo
typical: típico(a)

U

umbrella: guarda-chuva
uncle: tio
underline: sublinhar
understand: entender
unscramble: ordenar
use: usar
username: nome do usuário
usually: normalmente

V

vegetable: vegetal
version: versão
very: muito(a)
visually impaired person: cego(a)
vocabulary: vocabulário

W

walk: andar
wall: parede
wallet: carteira de dinheiro
wardrobe: guarda-roupas
warm: quente
warm-up: aquecimento
watch: assistir
water: água
watermelon: melancia
way: caminho, jeito
we: nós
weak: fraco(a)
wear: vestir
weather: tempo
weather forecast: previsão do tempo
weather man: metereologista
webcam: câmera
website: site (internet)
Wednesday: quarta-feira
week: semana
welcome: bem-vindo(a)
what: o que
wheelchair: cadeira de rodas
when: quando
whenever: quando (quer que)
where: onde
which: qual
white: branco(a)
who: quem
wholemeal: integral
whose: de quem, cujo(a)
why: por que
wide: largo(a)
window: janela
windy: ventoso
wing: asa
winter: inverno
with: com
woman: mulher
women: mulheres
wood: madeira
wool: lã
word: palavra
wordsearch: caça-palavras
work: trabalhar
world: mundo
write: escrever

X

Y

year: ano
yellow: amarelo(a)
you: você(s)
young: jovem
your: seu(s), sua(s)

Z

zoo: zoológico

Listening Script

Track 1 – Presentation

Track 2 – Unit 1, Listen, Exercise 1, page 8
David: Hi, I'm David.
Silvia: Hi, I'm Silvia.
Gabriela: Hello, everybody. My name's Gabriela.
Kazuki: Hello, my name's Kazuki. What's your name?

Track 3 – Unit 1 – Listen, Exercise 1, page 8
This is Ricardo./This is Sarah./This is Lyndon./This is Laura./This is Cate.

Track 4 – Unit 1, Speak, Exercise 1, page 9
Gabriela: I'm from Brazil. Where are you from?
Silvia: I'm from Brazil, too.
David: I'm from the USA.
Kazuki: I'm from Japan.

Track 5 – Unit 1, Speak, Exercise 2, page 9
Ricardo: Hi, I'm Ricardo and I'm from Brazil. Sarah is from England. Lyndon is from South Africa. Laura is from Argentina. Cate is from Australia.

Track 6 – Unit 2, Listen, Exercise 1a, page 18
When you need help.
Excuse me, how do you say "caneta" in English?
What does "book" mean?
Sorry, Can you repeat that, please?

Track 7 – Unit 2 – Listen, Exercise 1b, page 18
Language used in the classroom./Open your books./Close your books./Listen to the CD./Let's check the activity.

Track 8 – Unit 2, Listen, Exercise 2a, page 18
Kazuki: Are you ready?
Gabriela: No. Just a minute, please.

Track 9 – Unit 2, Listen, Exercise 2b, page 18
David: You go first. Ricardo: Ok, I'll go first.

Track 10 – Unit 2, Speak, Exercise 2 page 19
David: It's Tuesday today.
Ricardo: Yes. History class now. My favorite subject is history. What about you?
David: Use of Technology. I like computers, cell phones, tablets…
Ricardo: Tab… can you repeat, please?
David: Tablet.
Ricardo: Tablet. What does "tablet" mean?
David: It's a small portable computer with a touchscreen.
Ricardo: Oh, I see. Thanks for your help.
David: You're welcome.
Silvia: Ok, students! Open your books to page 10, exercise 2. Are you ready? Listen to the CD, please…

Track 11 – Unit 2, Speak, Exercise 3, page 19
Gabriela: What's your favorite subject, Kazuki?
Kazuki: My favorite subject is science. What about you?
Gabriela: My favorite subject is Portuguese.

Track 12 – Unit 2, Vocabulary, Exercise 2, page 21
1. a pencil case
2. a book
3. a brush
4. an umbrella
5. a bottle of water
6. tissues
7. a wallet
8. a notebook
9. a cap
10. a cell phone
11. a ruler
12. a pencil
13. a pen
14. an eraser
15. a calculator

Track 13 – Unit 3, Listen, exercise 1, page 30
Rooms at school
a) Principal's Office
b) Secretary's office
c) Teacher's room
d) Library
e) Computer lab
f) Music room
g) Science lab
h) Classroom
i) Boys' room
j) Girls'room
k) Gym
l) Art room
m) Cafeteria

Track 14 – Unit 3, Grammar Points, exercise 1, page 32
The alphabet
a – b – c – d – e – f – g – h – i – j – k – l – m – n – o – p – q – r – s – t – u – v – w – x – y – z

Track 15 – Unit 3, Grammar Points, Exercise 6, page 32
a) C-a-f-e-t-e-r-i-a
b) C-l-a-s-s-r-o-o-m
c) L-i-b-r-a-r-y
d) G-y-m

Track 16 – Unit 3, Vocabulary, Exercise 1, page 33
Numbers from 1 to 30
0 – oh/zero   1-one   2-two   3-three   4-four
5-five   6-six   7-seven   8-eight   9-nine   10-ten
11-eleven   12-twelve   13-thirteen   14-fourteen
15-fifteen   16-sixteen   17-seventeen   18-eighteen
19-nineteen   20-twenty   21-twenty-one
22-twenty-two   23-twenty-three   24- twenty-four
25-twenty-five   26-twenty-six   27-twenty-seven
28-twenty-eight   29-twenty-nine   30-thirty

Track 17 – Unit 3, Vocabulary, Exercise 4, page 33
Hi! My full name's Ricardo Andrade. My last name is A-N-D-R-A-D-E. I'm from Brazil. I'm in the sixth grade. My phone number is (41) 3417-9862.

Track 18 – Unit 4, Read, Exercise 4, page 39
Members of the family: grandparents, grandfather, grandmother, parents, father, mother, uncle, aunt, brother, sister.

Track 19 – Unit 4, Listen, Exercise 1, page 40
Gabriela: This is my family. This is my father. His name is Manoel. He's a math teacher.
Ricardo: Who's she?
Gabriela: She is my mother. Her name is Patricia. She's a dentist.
Kazuki: Who's this boy?
Gabriela: This is my brother. His name is Pedro. He's a student at ISB, too. And these are my grandparents Paulo and Tania.
Lyndon: Who's she?
Gabriela: She's my aunt Lúcia. She's an architect.

Track 20 – Unit 4, Listen, Exercise 2, page 40
a) a teacher   b) a student
c) an architect   d) a dentist

Track 21 – Unit 4, Vocabulary, Exercise 1, page 43
a) a doctor
b) a businesswoman
c) an engineer
d) a soccer player

Track 22 – Unit 5, Listen, Exercise 1, page 52
At the cafeteria

Kazuki: Are you okay, Ricardo?
Ricardo: No, I'm not.
Kazuki and Gabriela: Can we help you?
Ricardo: No, thank you.
Gabriela: Are you hungry?
Ricardo: No, I'm not.
Kazuki: Are you thirsty? What about an orange juice?
Ricardo: No, thanks.
Gabriela: So, what's the matter? You're not hungry, you're not thirsty…
Ricardo: My grades at school are my problems.

Track 23 – Unit 5, Speak, Exercise 1, page 53
Forty, fifty, sixty, seventy, eighty, ninety, a hundred or one hundred, a hundred and one or one hundred and one

Track 24 – Unit 5, Vocabulary, Exercise 1, page 56
Breakfast
Coffee , milk , bread , cheese , ham , orange juice
Lunch
Salad   French fries   rice and beans   vegetables
meat   chicken
Dinner
Soup   pizza   pasta   grilled fish   hot dog
Desserts
Pie   cupcake   fruit
Drinks
Tea   water   soda

Track 25 – Unit 5, Let's have fun, page 58
Colors: gray, white, yellow, red, green, orange, blue, black, brown, pink, purple.

Track 26 – Unit 6, Read, Exercise 3, page 62
Weather symbols: sunny, windy, rainy, snowy, cloudy, foggy

Track 27 – Unit 6, Listen, Exercise 1, page 63
This is Nic Farmer and this is his Monday weather report. Right now the temperature at the airport is twenty-seven degrees Celcius and the sky is clear. We couldn't ask for a better day for the first day of summer in Brazil. That's all for today's weather.

Track 28 – Unit 6, Listen, Exercise 2, page 63
Seasons of the year: summer is from December 21st to March 21st; fall is from March 21st to June 21st; winter is from June 21st to September 23rd; spring is from September 23rd to December 21st.

Track 29 – Unit 6, Speak, Exercise 4, page 64
Months of the year: January, February, March, April, May, June, July, August, September, October, November, December

Track 30 – Unit 6, Grammar Points, page 65
Ordinal numbers
First, second, third, fourth, fifth, sixth, seventh, eighth, ninth, tenth, eleventh, twelfth, thirteenth, fourteenth, fifteenth, sixteenth, seventeenth, eighteenth, nineteenth, twentieth, twenty-first, twenty-second, twenty-third, twenty-fourth, twenty-fifth, twenty-eighth, twenty-ninth, thirtieth

Track 31 – Unit 6, Vocabulary, Exercise 1, page 66
Clothes for hot weather: shorts, dress, T-shirt, skirt, blouse, cap, sneakers
Clothes for cold weather: jacket, coat, jeans, sweater, sweatpants, sweatshirt, socks

Track 32 – Unit 7, Read, Exercise 6, page 75
A shopping mall, a park, a zoo, a movie theater, a theater, a public library

Track 33 – Unit 7, Listen, Exercise 1, page 76
Kazuki: I'm hungry. Let's go to the Internet Café.
Gabriela: That's a good idea. But where is it?
Ricardo: It's on Second Street.
Gabriela: Is it across from the bank?
Kazuki: No, it isn't. It's next to the bank.

Track 34 – Unit 7, Listen, Exercise 2, page 76
Shopping mall, supermarket, fire station, coffee shop, museum, hospital, internet café, post office, restaurant, gas station, drugstore, movie theater, bookstore, park, bank, theater.

Track 35 – Unit 7, Grammar Points, Exercise 1, page 78
Gabriela: Is there a post office on Main Street?
Kazuki: Yes, there is.
Ricardo: Is there a bank on First Street?
Kazuki: No, there isn't. There's a bank on Second Street.
Gabriela: Are there any stores on Main Street?
Kazuki: Yes, there are. There is a drugstore and a bookstore.
Ricardo: Are there any restaurants on Park Avenue?
Kazuki: No, there aren't. There is a restaurant and a coffee shop on First Street.

Track 36 – Unit 7, Vocabulary, Exercise 1, page 79
Rooms in a house: bedroom, bathroom, living room, dining room, kitchen, garage

Track 37 – Unit 7, Vocabulary, Exercise 2, page 80
Furniture and appliances
A kitchen: a stove, a microwave, a refrigerator
A dining room: a table, a chair
A living room: a TV set, a sofa
A bedroom: a wardrobe, a desk, a bed
A bathroom: a toilet, a sink, a shower

Track 38 – Unit 8, Listen, Exercise 1, page 88
Extracurricular activities:
a) Sing and dance hip hop
b) Speak Chinese
c) Swim
d) Draw and paint
e) Play the guitar
f) Ride a horse

Track 39 – Unit 8, Speak, Exercise 4, page 89
a) He can't speak English.
b) She can swim.
c) We can dance.
d) I can't ride a horse.

Track 40 – Unit 8, Vocabulary, Exercise 2, page 91
Pets: a dog, a bird, a cat, a parrot, a fish, a rabbit

Track 41 – Unit 8, Write, Exercise 2, page 92
David: People use wheelchairs for many different reasons. If you're interacting with a student who is a wheelchair user for the first time, it can be difficult to know how to act. There are some tips you can follow to help people like me:
a) When you have a chat with a student in a wheelchair, sit down yourself, if it's possible keep eye to eye on the same level;
b) When you go to the cafeteria, try to identify a table that is easily accessible to a person who is using a wheelchair and keep a wide path open to it;
c) When changing rooms at school, check to see if the way to another room is accessible. Look for barriers that might be dangerous to getting into with wheelchairs;
d) It's okay for people who use wheelchairs to carry things on their laps. Many of us like to be able to reciprocate. So I can carry your backpack, your school bag or other things that are not too heavy. It's easier for me in the chair than for the person walking.

Track 42 – Reading is fun, page 139
The Real Princess by Hans Christian Andersen.

Reading is Fun

Before you read

WARM-UP: Are you from a royal family?

Do you like stories about kings and queens?

What is a real princess in your opinion?

Before you start reading, it's important to know some information about the author and where he was when he wrote the story. Do you know anything about Andersen?

1. **Read some facts about his life:**

   - He was from Denmark. (April 2rd, 1805 – August 4th, 1875)

   - He was an author, fairy tale writer, and poet noted for his children's stories.

   - Some books: "The Steadfast Tin Soldier", "The Snow Queen", "The Little Mermaid", "Thumbelina", and "The Ugly Duckling".

   - His poetry and stories have been translated into more than 150 languages.

2. **Now answer the questions:**

   a) A person from Denmark is _____.

   b) What are the names of "The Steadfast Tin Soldier" and "The Ugly Duckling" in Portuguese?

   _____

3. **Now listen and read the fairy tale.** TRACK 42

While you read

What kind of text is it?

Do you like fairy tales? If yes, what's your favorite fairy tale?

While you read the fairy tale, you'll read these words and expressions. What do they mean?

To be cast down – _____   Mattress – _____

Fearful tempest – _____   To be plain – _____

As dark as pitch – _____   Accordingly – _____

Trickle down – _____

The Real Princess

Hans Christian Andersen

There was once a Prince who wished to marry a Princess; but then she must be a real Princess. He travelled all over the world in hopes of finding such a lady; but there was always something wrong. Princesses he found in plenty; but whether they were real Princesses it was impossible for him to decide, for now one thing, now another, seemed to him not quite right about the ladies. At last he returned to his palace quite cast down, because he wished so much to have a real Princess for his wife. One evening a fearful tempest arose, it thundered and lightened, and the rain poured down from the sky in torrents: besides, it was as dark as pitch. All at once there was heard a violent knocking at the door, and the old King, the Prince's father, went out himself to open it. It was a Princess who was standing outside the door. What with the rain and the wind, she was in a sad condition; the water trickled down from her hair, and her clothes clung to her body. She said she was a real Princess.

"Ah! we shall soon see that!" thought the old Queen-mother; however, she said not a word of what she was going to do; but went quietly into the bedroom, took all the bed-clothes off the bed, and put three little peas on the bedstead. She then laid twenty mattresses one upon another over the three peas, and put twenty feather beds over the mattresses.

Upon this bed the Princess was to pass the night.

The next morning she was asked how she had slept. "Oh, very badly indeed!" she replied. "I have scarcely closed my eyes the whole night through. I do not know what was in my bed, but I had something hard under me, and am all over black and blue. It has hurt me so much!"

Now it was plain that the lady must be a real Princess, since she had been able to feel the three little peas through the twenty mattresses and twenty feather beds. None but a real Princess could have had such a delicate sense of feeling.

The Prince accordingly made her his wife; being now convinced that he had found a real Princess. The three peas were however put into the cabinet of curiosities, where they are still to be seen, provided they are not lost.

Wasn't this a lady of real delicacy?

From Andersen's Fairy Tales. Available at: <www.dominiopublico.gov.br/download/texto/gu001597.pdf>. Access on: Jun. 27th, 2011.

After you read

4. Look at the pictures. Try to find in the text the sentences that correspond to the pictures.

Princesses he found in plenty.

5. Answer the questions about the story.

   a) What's the title of the story?
   The Real Princess.

   b) Who are the characters in the story?
   _____

   c) How was the weather in the story when the princess arrived in the palace?
   _____

   d) Who opened the door for the princess?
   _____

   e) Who put the three little peas on the bedstead?
   _____

   f) How many mattresses and feather beds were there?
   _____

6. Find words in the text which mean the opposite of the words below. If it's necessary, look at the dictionary.

   a) right _____   b) insufficiently _____
   c) fearless _____   d) impossible _____
   e) false _____   f) bright _____
   g) peaceful _____   h) happy _____
   i) big _____   j) well _____
   k) noisily _____   l) rough _____

7. Are the sentences true (T) or false (F) according to the story?

   a) The Prince wished to marry a real Princess. (**T**)
   b) He traveled all over the United States in hopes of finding such a lady. (   )
   c) The weather was sunny, hot and windy. (   )
   d) The Princess was in a very sad condition when she arrived at the palace. (   )
   e) The Princess slept very well. (   )
   f) The Princess was very delicate. (   )

141

8. Match the correct parts of the sentences.

(1) I do not know what was in my bed,
(2) At last he returned to his palace quite cast down,
(3) The three peas were however put into the cabinet of curiosities,
(4) None but a real Princess
(5) Upon this bed
(6) The Prince accordingly made her his wife;
(7) There was once a Prince who wished to marry a Princess;

(   ) could have had such a delicate sense of feeling.
(   ) being now convinced that he had found a real Princess.
(   ) because he wished so much to have a real Princess for his wife.
(1) but I had something hard under me, and am all over black and blue.
(   ) the Princess was to pass the night.
(   ) but then she must be a real Princess.
(   ) where they are still to be seen, provided they are not lost.

9. Who are they?

Who…?

a) wished to marry a Princess? **The Prince.**
b) traveled around the world to find a Princess? _____
c) knocked at the door violently? _____
d) went quietly into the bedroom? _____
e) asked the Princess how she had slept? _____
f) scarcely closed the eyes the whole night through? _____

10. Exchanging ideas. Talk with your classmates about the questions below.

a) Do you think the prince's mother should have believed in the princess's words?
_____

b) Why in your opinion would the prince like to marry a real princess?
_____

c) Do you think that the kind of blood people have makes a difference in people's attitudes?
_____

References

ARATANGY, Lidia Rosenberg. **Adolescentes na era digital**. São Paulo: Benvirá, 2011.

BOWEN, Philippa; CUMINO, Margherita. **Cultural links. An exploration of the English-speaking world**. Canterbury: Black Cat, 2010.

CLEARY, Maria. **Talking culture**. Helbling Languages, 2006.

CORBETT, John. **Intercultural Language Activities**. Cambridge: Cambridge University Press, 2010.

EVANS, Linda; BACKUS, Karen; THOMPSON, Mary. **Art projects from around the world**. New York: Scholastic, 2006.

FREIRE, Paulo. **Pedagogy of the oppressed**. New York: Longman, 1989.

GILBERT, Judy B. **Clear speech**. New York: Cambridge University Press, 1993.

GILL, Simon; CANKOVA, Michaela. **Intercultural activities**. Oxford: OUP, 2008.

GODOY, Sonia M. Baccari de. **English pronunciation for Brazilians**. Barueri: Disal Editora, 2006.

LAPKOSKI, Graziella Araujo de Oliveira. **Do texto ao sentido:** teoria e prática de leitura em língua inglesa. Curitiba: IBPEX, 2011.

LIEFF, Camilla Dixo; POW, Elizabeth M.; NUNES, Zaina Abdalla. **Descobrindo a pronúncia do Inglês**. São Paulo: Martins Fontes, 2010.

MARCUSCHI, Luiz Antônio. **Os desafios da identificação do gênero textual nas atividades de ensino: propósitos comunicativos *versus* forma estrutural**. III SIGET – Simpósio Internacional de Estudos dos Gêneros Textuais. Universidade Federal de Santa Maria, Santa Maria, 16-18 agosto de 2005.

SAMPEDRO, Ricardo; HILLYARD, Susan. **Global issues**. Oxford: Oxford University Press, 2004.

SCHOENBERG, Irene E. **Focus on grammar:** an integrated skills approach. 3rd Ed. New York: Pearson Education, 2006.

SCHOLES, Jack. **Break the branch?** São Paulo: Disal Editora, 2008.

_____. **Why do we say that?** São Paulo: Elsevier Editora, 2009.

SCHUMACHER, Cristina; WHITE, Philip de Lacy; ZANETTINI, Marta. **Guia de pronúncia do inglês para brasileiros**. São Paulo: Elsevier Editora Ltda, 2002.

SECRETARIA DE EDUCAÇÃO FUNDAMENTAL. Língua Estrangeira, Parâmetros Curriculares Nacionais. Brasília, DF: Ministério da Educação, 1998.

SOUZA, Adriana Grade Fiori Souza; ABSY, Conceição A.; COSTA, Gisele Cilli da; MELLO, Leonilde Favoreto de. **Leitura em Língua Inglesa**. Barueri: Disal Editora, 2005.

UNDERHILL, A. **Sound foundations:** living phonology. Oxford: Heinemann English Language Teaching, 1994.

VYGOTSKY, Lev Semionovitch. **A formação social da mente**. São Paulo: Martins Fontes, 1989.

_____. **Pensamento e Linguagem**. São Paulo: Martins Fontes Editora, 1991.

WALESKO, Angela Maria Hoffmann. **Compreensão oral em língua inglesa**. Curitiba: IBPEX, 2010.

ZIMMER, Márcia; SILVEIRA, Rosane; ALVES, Ubiratã Kickhöfel. **Pronunciation Instruction for Brazilians**. Newcastle upon Tyne: Cambridge Scholars Publishing, 2009.

DICTIONARIES

Collins Cobuild Advanced Learner's English Dictionary, Fourth Edition, Glasgow: HarperCollins Publishers, 2005.

The Merriam-Webster Collegiate Dictionary Eleventh Edition, 2007

The Merriam-Webster Dictionary of Quotations. Merriam-Webster, INC., Publishers Springfield, Massachusetts, 1992.

The Penguin Dictionary of Language. David Crystal, 1999.

Oxford Concise Dictionary of Linguistics. P.H.Matthews, 2005.

Oxford Guide to British and American Culture, 2000.

Oxford Advanced Learner's Dictionary, 7th Edition. Oxford: OUP, 2005.

The Wordsworth Dictionary of British History. J.P.Kenyon, 1994.